MW01485874

MY GOATS...

_____

_____

_____

_____

_____

_____

_____

_____

_____

_____

A LIFE OF HERITAGE

...your life of heritage

www.alifeofheritage.com

MY HERD NAME

_____

MY NAME

_____

MY GOAT BINDER

TABLE OF CONTENTS

goat's name

_____

Registration #: _____

Sex: _____ # in Birth: _____

Date of Birth: _____

Sire & Registration #:_____

Dam & Registration #:_____

State Born: _____

Tattoo & Date: RE:_____ LE:_____

Castration Date: _____ Disbudding Date:_____

Color: _____

_____

Transfer Records:_____

Notes:_____

_____

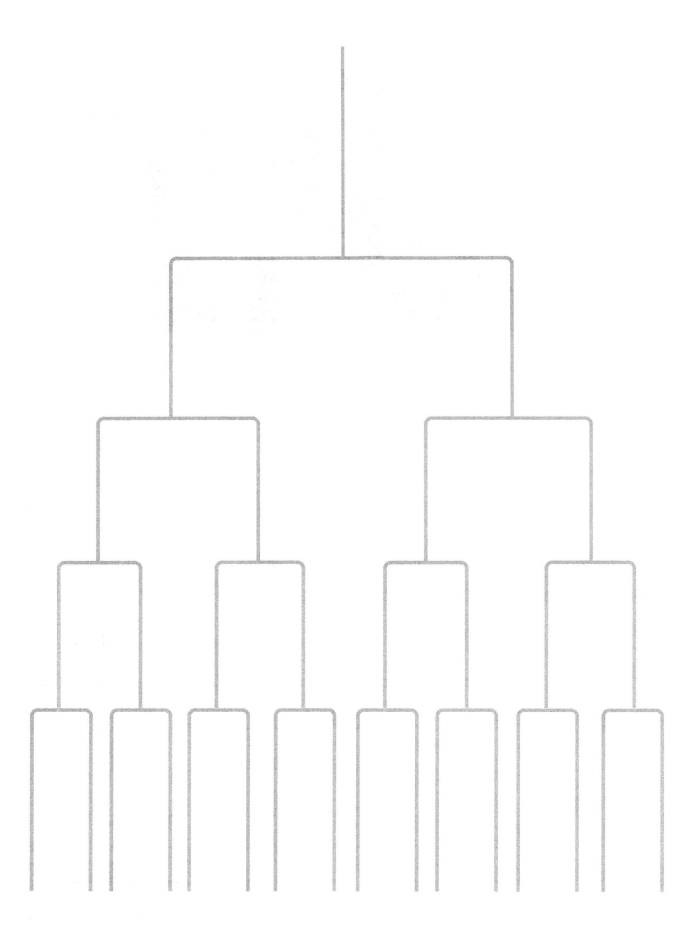

YEARLY
GOAT HEALTH
TRACKING

	TEMP/ PULSE	RESP/ RUMEN	FAMACHA SCORE	FECAL COUNT	WORMED/ DOSAGE	HOOF TRIM	COPPER BOLUS	BO-SE SHOT	VACCINES
1ST Q JAN									
FEB									
MAR									
2ND Q APR									
MAY									
JUN									
3RD Q JUL									
AUG									
SEPT									
4TH Q OCT									
NOV									
DEC									

NAME: _____

REGISTRATION #: _____

NOTES: _____

 20__

YEARLY
BUCK PERFORMANCE
RECORDS

BREEDING DATE	DOE NAME/ ID	TOTAL OFF-SPRING	SEX	COMMENTS

NOTES: _____
_____
_____
_____
_____

➡ 20__

goat's name

Registration #: _____

Sex: _____ # in Birth: _____

Date of Birth: _____

Sire & Registration #:_____

Dam & Registration #: _____

State Born: _____

Tattoo & Date: RE: _____ LE: _____

Castration Date: _____ Disbudding Date: _____

Color: _____
_____

Transfer Records:_____

Notes:_____
_____

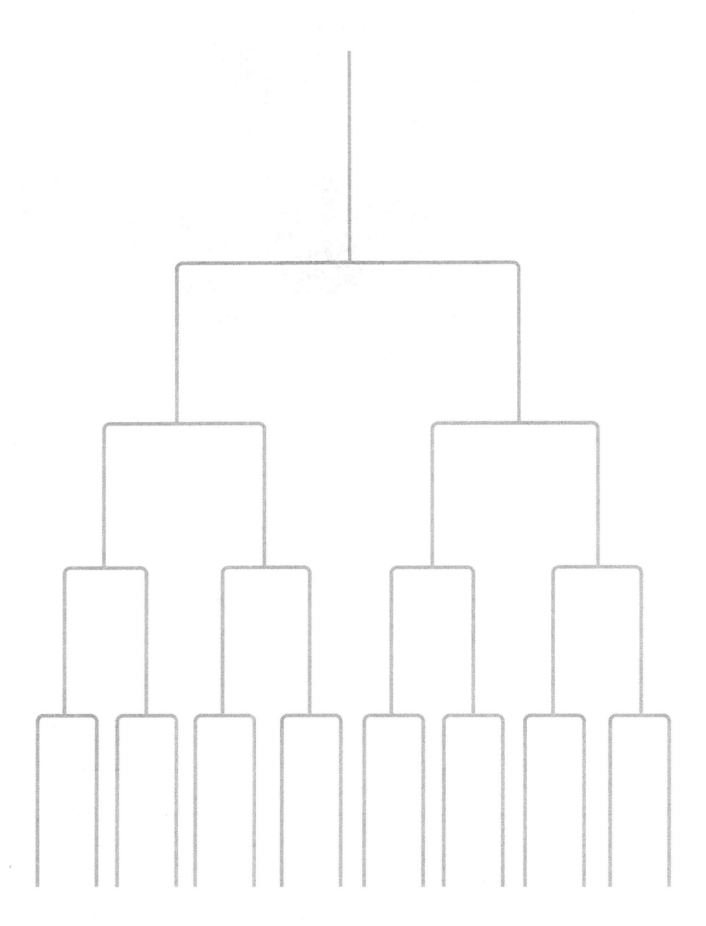

YEARLY
GOAT HEALTH
TRACKING

	TEMP/ PULSE	RESP/ RUMEN	FAMACHA SCORE	FECAL COUNT	WORMED/ DOSAGE	HOOF TRIM	COPPER BOLUS	BO-SE SHOT	VACCINES
1ST Q JAN									
FEB									
MAR									
2ND Q APR									
MAY									
JUN									
3RD Q JUL									
AUG									
SEPT									
4TH Q OCT									
NOV									
DEC									

NAME: _____

REGISTRATION #: _____

NOTES: _____

➡ 20__

YEARLY
GOAT REPRODUCTION
TRACKING

	HEAT CYCLE	BUCK NAME	BUCK TURNED IN/OUT	BRED ON	ULTRA SOUND	PREG?	DRY OFF	DUE DATE	MOVE TO KIDDING STALL	STALL #	# IN BIRTH	WEAN DATE
1ST Q JAN	IN: OUT:											
FEB	IN: OUT:											
MAR	IN: OUT:											
2ND Q APR	IN: OUT:											
MAY	IN: OUT:											
JUN	IN: OUT:											
3RD Q JUL	IN: OUT:											
AUG	IN: OUT:											
SEPT	IN: OUT:											
4TH Q OCT	IN: OUT:											
NOV	IN: OUT:											
DEC	IN: OUT:											

NOTES: _____
_____
_____
_____

➡️ 20__

YEARLY
DOE PERFORMANCE
RECORDS

BREED DATE	BUCK NAME/ ID	TOTAL OFF-SPRING	SEX	COMMENTS

NAME: _____

REGISTRATION #: _____

NOTES: _____

_____

YEARLY
DOE PERFORMANCE
RECORDS

BREED DATE	BUCK NAME/ ID	TOTAL OFF- SPRING	SEX	COMMENTS

GOAT REPRODUCTION
TRACKING

BIRTH DATE	# IN BIRTH	DOES	BUCKS	PREGNANCY NOTES	DELIVERY NOTES	OFFSPRING NOTES

NAME: _____

REGISTRATION #: _____

NOTES: _____

_____

GOAT REPRODUCTION

TRACKING

BIRTH DATE	# IN BIRTH	DOES	BUCKS	PREGNANCY NOTES	DELIVERY NOTES	OFFSPRING NOTES

KID NAME/ ID/BREED/DOE	BIRTH DATE	LITTER SIZE	SEX	BIRTH WEIGHT	30 DAY WEIGHT	60 DAY WEIGHT	90 DAY WEIGHT	WEANING AGE & WEIGHT

YEARLY
KIDDING
RECORDS ➡ 20__

KID NAME/ID/BREED/DOE	BIRTH DATE	LITTER SIZE	SEX	BIRTH WEIGHT	30 DAY WEIGHT	60 DAY WEIGHT	90 DAY WEIGHT	WEANING AGE & WEIGHT

MONTHLY
GOAT MILK
RECORDS

 20__

MONTH	NAME MILK YIELD		NAME MILK YIELD		NAME MILK YIELD		OUTSIDE TEMP	COMMENTS
	AM	PM	AM	PM	AM	PM		
1								
2								
3								
4								
5								
6								
7								
8								
9								
10								
11								
12								
13								
14								
15								
16								
17								
18								
19								
20								
21								
22								
23								
24								
25								
26								
27								
28								
29								
30								
31								

MONTHLY
GOAT MILK
RECORDS

 20__

MONTH	NAME MILK YIELD		NAME MILK YIELD		NAME MILK YIELD		OUTSIDE TEMP	COMMENTS
	AM	PM	AM	PM	AM	PM		
1								
2								
3								
4								
5								
6								
7								
8								
9								
10								
11								
12								
13								
14								
15								
16								
17								
18								
19								
20								
21								
22								
23								
24								
25								
26								
27								
28								
29								
30								
31								

MY GOAT
TEST
RESULTS

GOAT:

DATE	TEST	RESULTS

MY GOAT
TEST
RESULTS

GOAT:

DATE	TEST	RESULTS

MY GOAT
TREATMENT PLAN

GOAT:

DATE	CLINICAL SIGNS	DIAGNOSIS	TREATMENT PLAN & DURATION	DOSAGE & ROUTE OF ADMIN
1-21	SEVERE DIARRHEA WEIGHT LOSS WHITE GUMS	COCCIDIOSIS DIARRHEA ANEMIC	ALBON 1/21-1.26 KAOPECTATE UNTIL STOPS RED CELL 1/21-1/1/27	ALBON 8 OZ/15 GAL OF WATER, ORALLY KAOPECTATE 7 CC ORALLY RED CELL 5 CC ORALLY DAILY

MY GOAT
TREATMENT PLAN

GOAT:

DATE	CLINICAL SIGNS	DIAGNOSIS	TREATMENT PLAN & DURATION	DOSAGE & ROUTE OF ADMIN

QUICK GLANCE
GOAT HERD
INVENTORY

GOAT NAME, REGISTRATION # & BREED	BIRTH DATE	SEX	VALUE OF ANIMAL	NOTES

PURCHASE ▪ SELLING ▪ DEATH RECORDS
GOAT HERD
TRACKING

GOAT NAME, REGISTRATION # & BREED	PURCHASE DATE & DETAILS	SELLING DATE & DETAILS	DEATH DATE & DETAILS

REPLACEMENT RECORDS
GOAT HERD
INVENTORY

GOAT NAME, REGISTRATION #, TAG # & BREED	BIRTH DATE	SEX	WEANING DATE	VALUE OF ANIMAL	NOTES

CULL RECORDS
GOAT HERD
INVENTORY

GOAT NAME, REGISTRATION #, TAG # & BREED	BIRTH DATE	SEX	REASON FOR CULLING	METHOD OF CULLING	NOTES

YEARLY
FEED INVENTORY → 20__

DATE	TYPE OF FEED	COST/ITEM	QUANTITY	TOTAL COST

YEARLY
HAY INVENTORY → 20__

DATE	HAY DETAILS	COST/TON COST/BALE	(QUANTITY) TON/ BALES	TOTAL COST

YEARLY
GOAT SALES 20__

DATE OF SALE	NAME TAG/REGISTRATION #	BREED	DATE OF BIRTH	SEX	PRICE SOLD FOR	BUYER

YEARLY
MILK SALES

➡ 20__

DATE OF SALE	AMOUNT IN GALLONS	PRICE SOLD FOR	PICKUP DETAILS	BUYER

REPUTABLE BREEDERS

NAME/ BUSINESS NAME	CONTACT INFO	BREED	NOTES/ BUY AGAIN?
			YES / NO
			YES / NO
			YES / NO
			YES / NO
			YES / NO
			YES / NO
			YES / NO

REPUTABLE BREEDERS

NAME/ BUSINESS NAME	CONTACT INFO	BREED	NOTES/ BUY AGAIN?
			YES / NO
			YES / NO
			YES / NO
			YES / NO
			YES / NO
			YES / NO
			YES / NO

VENDOR & SUPPLY LIST

VENDOR/ BUSINESS NAME	CONTACT INFO	SUPPLIES	NOTES/ BUY AGAIN?
			YES / NO
			YES / NO
			YES / NO
			YES / NO
			YES / NO
			YES / NO
			YES / NO

VENDOR & SUPPLY LIST

VENDOR/ BUSINESS NAME	CONTACT INFO	SUPPLIES	NOTES/ BUY AGAIN?
			YES / NO
			YES / NO
			YES / NO
			YES / NO
			YES / NO
			YES / NO
			YES / NO

EMERGENCY PLAN

VETERINARY SERVICE
_____
_____

VET'S NAME
_____
_____

VET'S PHONE NUMBER
_____

BLOOD TRANSFUSION CONTACT INFORMATION
_____
_____

LOCAL LAB
_____
_____

LOCAL LAB (MASTITIS)
_____
_____

EMERGENCY PLAN

ASSUME ALL WILL BE WELL BUT BE READY FOR WHEN IT'S NOT!
MAKE THE HARD DECISIONS NOW SO YOU WON'T HAVE TO UNDER STRESS.

LOCAL EVACUATION LOCAL FIRE, FLOOD, ETC

_____

_____

TRANSPORTATION

_____

_____

SEVERE WEATHER

TORNADO

_____

HURRICANE

_____

HAIL

_____

HEAT ADVISORIES

_____

SEVERE WINTER

_____

OTHER

_____

EMERGENCY PLAN

ASSUME ALL WILL BE WELL BUT BE READY FOR WHEN IT'S NOT!
MAKE THE HARD DECISIONS NOW SO YOU WON'T HAVE TO UNDER STRESS.

KIDDING COMPLICATIONS

CALL VET?   Y   N   C-SECTION   Y   N

VACCINATIONS

YEARLY VACCINATIONS (CDT & TETNUS)   Y   N
TETANUS ANTITOXIN ON HAND?   Y   N

BLOOD TRANSFUSION

WHAT WILL YOU DO IF YOUR GOAT NEEDS A BLOOD TRANSFUSION?
I.E. IN THE CASE OF SEVERE ANEMIA.   TRANSFUSION   Y   N

_____

BROKEN BONES

WHAT WILL YOU DO IF YOUR GOAT BREAKS A LEG AND NEEDS A CAST?

CAST?   Y   N

_____

DISEASE

WHAT WILL YOU DO IF YOUR GOAT CONTRACTS A CONTAGIOUS, NON-CURABLE DISEASE?

_____

_____

EMERGENCY PLAN

ASSUME ALL WILL BE WELL BUT BE READY FOR WHEN IT'S NOT!
MAKE THE HARD DECISIONS NOW SO YOU WON'T HAVE TO UNDER STRESS.

KID COMPLICATIONS

WHAT WILL YOU DO IF A KID IS BORN WITH DEFICIENCIES AND IT BECOMES
EVIDENT THAT HE WON'T PULL OUT OF IT AND RECOVER?

_____

_____

NECROPSY AFTER DEATH

WILL YOU ASK YOUR VET FOR A NECROPSY AFTER A GOAT'S DEATH,
WHEN YOU DON'T KNOW WHY IT DIED?

NECROPSY?   Y   N

_____

_____

RELOCATION

WHERE WILL YOUR GOATS GO IN THE EVENT THAT YOU CAN NO LONGER
CARE FOR THEM?

_____

_____

OTHER

_____

_____

_____

_____

_____

GOAT CARE
RECIPES

MOLASSES WATER

→ 1/4-1/2 cup molasses
→ 1 cup hot water
→ 1 gallon water

Mix molasses with the one cup of hot water well. Add this mixture to the gallon of water. Offer this to a doe after birth and for any goat needing some quick energy.

GOAT MILK REPLACER

→ 1 gallon of whole cow's milk
→ 1 cup cultured buttermilk
→ 1 can of evaporated milk

OPTIONAL
→ 5 cc Nutridrench
(add to bottles every few days)

Mix ingredients together well. Store in refrigerator. Shake well before each use. Warm slowly to desired temperature. Feed to baby goats.

*If at all possible, find fresh goat milk to feed to kids, or use powdered goat milk replacer. This can be used as an alternative if no goat milk can be located. Don't switch back and forth between options.

ELECTROLYTES

→ 3-4 qts of warm water
→ 2 tsp salt
→ 2 tsp baking soda
→ 1/2 cup molasses

OPTIONAL:
(these may make it less appealing)

→ Up to 1 cup apple cider vinegar
→ And/or 5cc Nutri-Drench

Mix all of these ingredients together in a jug or bucket and give free choice or drench your sick goat.
It's best to use within 24 hours and make a new batch each day.

EASY UDDER WASH

→ Water filled spray bottle
→ Just enough iodine to turn the water reddish colored

Mix water and iodine and keep in a spray bottle to clean your goat's udder before milking.

KIDDING KIT
ESSENTIALS

GOAT OWNER PREPARATION

- [ ] Barn, preferably with light
- [ ] Goat shelters
- [ ] Goat pen
- [ ] Straw or Shavings (Bedding)
- [ ] Feed: Hay & Grain
- [ ] Vet's phone number
- [ ] Read up on hypocalcemia, ketosis and pregnancy toxemia so you know the signs and symptoms that might appear so you can act quickly. They affect pregnant does and are not something to mess with!

THE KID(S) AFTER BIRTH

- [ ] Bulb Syringe
- [ ] Puppy Training Pads
- [ ] Paper Towels/Rags
- [ ] Towels
- [ ] Floss or Clamps
- [ ] Scissors
- [ ] Small Container
- [ ] 7% Iodine Tincture
- [ ] Kid Colostrum Replacement
- [ ] Bottle & Nipple
- [ ] Weak Lamb Syringe
- [ ] Thermometer
- [ ] Warming Hut

WHEN GOAT IS IN LABOR

- [ ] Flashlight
- [ ] Standard Medical Gloves
- [ ] Warm Water
- [ ] Surgical Scrub
- [ ] OB Lube & Betadine
- [ ] Obstetric (OB) Gloves
- [ ] Leg Snare or Kid Puller
- [ ] Empty Feed Sacks
- [ ] Scissors
- [ ] 7% Iodine Tincture
- [ ] Thermometer
- [ ] Drench Gun
- [ ] Twine (to braid and keep yourself busy with)
- [ ] _____
- [ ] _____

THE DOE AFTER BIRTH

- [ ] Molasses Water
- [ ] Grain

CAMERA!

Tracking
GOAT PREGNANCY
Personalized Dates

MARK YOUR CALENDAR WITH EACH OF THESE IMPORTANT DATES!

BREEDING DATE

DUE DATE

BEGINNING OF PREGNANCY

- NO DRUGS IN 1ST 30 DAYS
- PROVIDE GOOD QUALITY HAY
- PROVIDE LOOSE MINERAL
- STRESS FREE ENVIRONMENT

NO DRUGS DATES

MIDDLE OF PREGNANCY

TWO MONTHS BEFORE DUE DATE

- STOP MILKING
- START FEEDING ALFALFA HAY
- START FEEDING 15% PROTIEN GRAIN CONCENTRATE
- DAILY MONITOR YOUR GOAT
- WATCH FOR SIGNS OF PREGNANCY TOXEMIA & HYPOCALCEMIA

2 MONTH BEFORE KIDDING DATE

END OF PREGNANCY

VACCINATE & MEDICATE

- CD&T (4 WEEKS BEFORE DUE DATE)
- WORM (1 WEEK BEFORE DUE DATE)

CDT DATE WORMING DATE

FIRST GOAT ESSENTIALS

FENCING OPTIONS

→ Pallets
→ Sheep/Cattle Panels
→ Woven Wire
→ Electric Fence
→ Other Options:

_____

_____

SHELTER

→ Your goats will need shelter from the rain, snow, wind and elements. This could be as simple as a shelter made from pallets or a completely enclosed, large barn.

→ Bedding: Straw or Pine Shavings

IMPORTANT REMINDERS

- *If you have multiple pens, plan out how two pens can share one water trough.*
- *Keep hay off the ground as much as possible, this will help limit worms.*
- *If you are bringing home a buck, the fencing you have between the does and bucks should be put together well and secure enough to keep them apart. Consider electric wire at the top to discourage jumping and climbing over.*
- *Think long-term, will you be having kids in the future? You will need a separate area to wean them. Think ahead and plan for it as you are building fences now.*

HOOF TRIMMING SUPPLIES

→ Gloves
→ Hoof Trimmers
→ Hoof Pick with Brush
→ Hoof Plane
→ Hoof'n Heal: heals all types of hoof injury

IMPORTANT REMINDERS

- *When trimming hooves, wear gloves! A quick jerk can put a hole in your finger!*
- *Purchase trimmers specifically for goats*
- *Trim hooves regularly. Trim at least quarterly. Poop + dirt + overgrown hooves lead to disease and sickness.*

FIRST GOAT ESSENTIALS

FOOD & WATER

→ Water Trough or Buckets
→ Hose
→ Feeder
→ Grain Dish
→ Feed: Hay & Grain
→ Measuring Cup or Scoop
→ _____

SUPPLIES

→ Wormer
→ Oral Syringe for Drenching
→ Collars and Leashes
→ Brushes
→ Clippers
→ Rectal Thermometer
→ _____

IMPORTANT REMINDERS

- *Changing a goat's diet quickly can cause them to bloat and have very serious consequences.*

VITAMINS & MINERALS

→ Loose Mineral
→ Baking Soda
→ Salt
→ Mineral, Baking Soda, & Salt Dispensers

MILKING SUPPLIES

→ Milking Stand
→ Stainless Steal Milking Bucket
→ Funnel & Strainer (to strain milk into glass containers for consumption)
→ Milk Filters
→ Glass Jars/Containers for Storage
→ Mastitis Tests
→ _____

"Success is where preparation and opportunity meet."
Prepare for Goat + Find Goat = SUCCESS!

GOAT HEALTH AT A GLANCE

TEMPERATURE
101.5°-103°

FULL GROWTH SIZE:
GOATS WILL CONTINUE TO GROW INTO THEIR 3RD YEAR

LIFE SPAN:
DOES: 11-12 YEARS ON AVERAGE, DEATH IS USUALLY KIDDING RELATED. DOES WHO RETIRE FROM BREEDING, AROUND THE AGE OF TEN, LIVE LONGER (16-18 YEARS.)

BUCKS: 8-10 YEARS, THE STRESSES OF GOING INTO RUT EACH YEAR CAUSE THEIR LIFESPAN TO BE SHORTER

WETHERS: 11-16 YEARS ON AVERAGE

PULSE
70-80 BEATS/MINUTE

GESTATION:
143-155 DAYS

RESPIRATORY
15-30/MINUTE

ESTRUS/HEAT CYCLE:
17-23 DAYS

RUMEN MOVEMENTS
1-1.5/MINUTE

WEAN BUCKS AT 2 MONTHS AND SEPARATE FROM DOES

PUBERTY
7 WEEKS TO 8 MONTHS

TAKING TEMPERATURE

HOW TO

HOW TO TAKE A GOAT'S TEMPERATURE

→ CLEAN THERMOMETER THOROUGHLY

→ ADD LUBRICANT TO TIP OF THERMOMETER

→ INSERT INTO RECTUM, HOLD STEADY UNTIL BEEP OR FOR 60 SECONDS

→ CLEAN THERMOMETER THOROUGHLY & PUT AWAY!

REASONS

REASONS FOR A TEMPERATURE

→ **HIGH TEMP:** INFECTION OR DEHYDRATION

→ **LOW TEMP**: INTERNAL ORGANS ARE SHUTTING DOWN! ACT QUICKLY!

→ **USE FIVE SENSES**: SEE, HEAR, TOUCH, TASTE, SMELL

WHEN

TAKE TEMPERATURE WHEN...

→ GOAT OFF BY ITSELF

→ ABNORMAL POOP

→ BLOATED RUMEN

→ RUMEN NOT GURGLING

→ OFF TASTING MILK

→ GOAT IN PAIN, MOANING

→ DEPRESSED, DROOPING TAIL AND HEAD

→ ANY SIGN OF SICKNESS

GOAT WEIGHT

OPTION 1

YOU CAN USE A CHART LIKE THIS ONE TO DETERMINE WHAT YOUR GOAT WEIGHS. YOU ONLY NEED TO MEASURE THE GOAT'S GIRTH AND IT IS ACCURATE WITHIN A COUPLE OF POUNDS.

HEART GIRTH (IN)	WEIGHT (LBS)	HEART GIRTH (IN)	WEIGHT (LBS)	HEART GIRTH (IN)	WEIGHT (LBS)
10 3/4	5	20	30	32	100
11 3/4	6	21	34	33	105
12 3/4	7	22	38	34	115
13 1/4	8	23	43	35	125
13 3/4	9	24	50	36	140
14 1/4	10	25	56	37	150
14 3/4	11	26	62	38	160
15 1/4	12	27	68	39	170
16	14	28	73	40	180
17	16	29	80	41	190
18	22	30	85	42	200
19	26	31	90	43	215

OPTION 2

USING A SEWING MEASURING TAPE: MEASURE, BY PULLING TIGHTLY AROUND THE GIRTH (BEHIND THE WITHERS AND BEHIND THE FRONT LEGS, WHERE THE HEART IS LOCATED). ALSO, MEASURE THE LENGTH OF THE ANIMAL. FROM THE POINT OF THE SHOULDER TO THE PIN BONE (THE BONES BESIDE THE TAIL). PUT THE NUMBERS INTO THE GOAT WEIGHT CALCULATOR BELOW AND YOU HAVE YOUR ANSWER!

HEART GIRTH X HEART GIRTH X BODY LENGTH = TOTAL / 300 = ANIMAL WEIGHT IN LBS

OPTION 3

USE A BATHROOM SCALE:
YOU WOULD WEIGH YOURSELF FIRST, WRITE DOWN THE MEASUREMENTS AND THEN WEIGH YOU AND THE GOAT TOGETHER. THE DIFFERENCE BETWEEN THE NUMBERS IS THE WEIGHT OF YOUR GOAT.

HOOF TRIMMING

HOW TO

HOW TO TRIM A GOAT'S HOOVES

 CLEAN DIRT FROM SOLE & FROM BETWEEN TOES
- USE POINT OF TRIMMER TO CLEAN OUT DIRT

 TRIM THE OUTER WALL
- IF OVERGROWN, PRY OPEN AND CAREFULLY CUT THE OVERGROWN HOOF WALL. CUT IN SMALL PIECES TO AVOID CUTTING TOO DEEP.
- ALWAYS STOP TRIMMING WHEN THE SOLE APPEARS PINKISH.
- TRIM OFF ALL HOOF ROT UNTIL IT HAS BEEN REMOVED. HOOF ROT IS NORMALLY FOUND NEAR THE TIP OF THE TOE AND ALONG THE HOOF WALLS; IT SELDOM OCCURS AT THE HEEL.
- KEEP BOTH KOPERTOX AND BLOOD STOP POWDER HANDY TO HELP IF ANY BLOOD APPEARS WHEN A HOOF IS CUT TOO DEEP.

 TRIM BETWEEN THE HOOVES
- TRIM EXCESS HOOF WALL BETWEEN THE TOES AND WHERE THE HEELS MEET.

 TRIM HEEL
- REMEMBER, THE HEELS ARE SOFTER THAN ANY OTHER PART OF THE HOOF. IF IN DOUBT ABOUT WHAT A GOAT'S HOOF SHOULD LOOK LIKE, EXAMINE A VERY YOUNG KID'S HOOF.

 TRIM DEWCLAWS
- IF NEEDED, TRIM THE DEWCLAWS ONE SMALL SNIP AT A TIME.

IN AREAS WITH CONSIDERABLE RAINFALL, CONSIDER PLACING FOOT BATHS IN AREAS THAT THE GOATS WOULD HAVE TO WALK THROUGH EACH DAY. THESE WOULD HAVE COPPER SULFATE IN THEM AND THEN AN AREA WHERE THEY CAN WALK THROUGH DIATOMACEOUS EARTH, WHICH IS USED AS A DRYING AGENT. THIS HELPS PREVENT HOOF ROT AND HOOF SCALD. AND TETANUS SHOTS WOULD PREVENT TETANUS IF A HOOF WAS OPENED UP.

HOOF TRIMMING

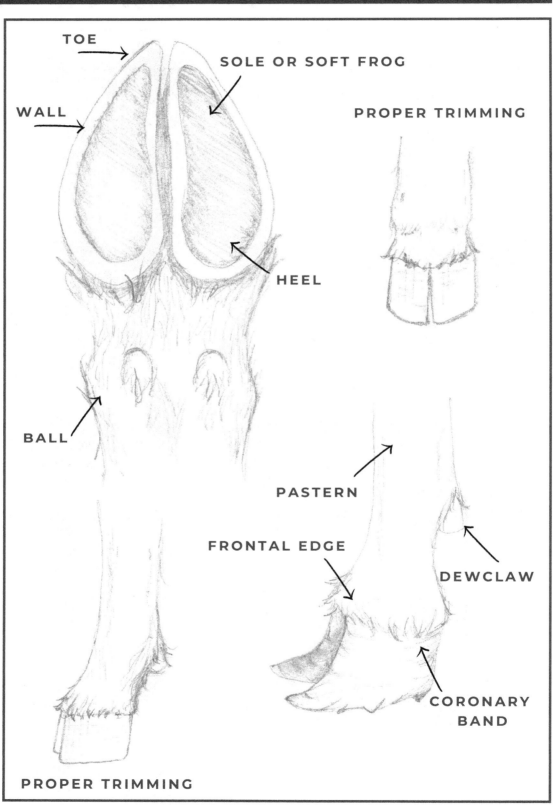

TOE

SOLE OR SOFT FROG

PROPER TRIMMING

WALL

HEEL

BALL

PASTERN

FRONTAL EDGE

DEWCLAW

CORONARY BAND

PROPER TRIMMING

HOOF TRIMMING

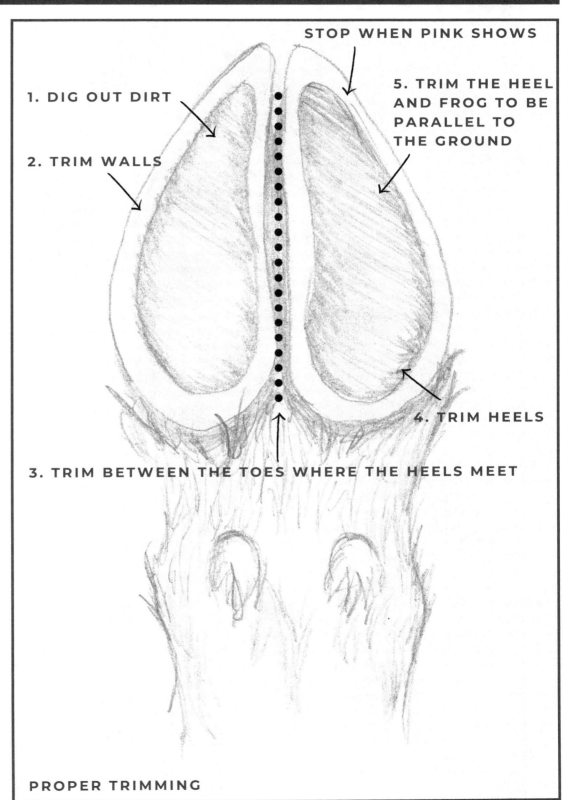

1. DIG OUT DIRT

2. TRIM WALLS

STOP WHEN PINK SHOWS

5. TRIM THE HEEL AND FROG TO BE PARALLEL TO THE GROUND

4. TRIM HEELS

3. TRIM BETWEEN THE TOES WHERE THE HEELS MEET

PROPER TRIMMING

DISBUDDING

HOW TO DISBUD A GOAT KID

HOW TO

→ AROUND 10-14 DAYS (NO LATER!)

→ PLACE KID IN DEHORNING BOX OR HOLD FIRMLY UNDER YOU

→ HEAT DEHORNING IRON TO RED HOT

- THE IRON CAN BE TESTED ON A PIECE OF WOOD AND SHOULD LEAVE A BURNED RING WHEN IT IS HOT ENOUGH

→ PLACE IRON AROUND HORN AND TURN

→ POP OFF THE TIP OF THE HORN WITH THUMB OR KNIFE

→ PLACE THE IRON IN THE SAME PLACE AND SLOWLY TURN UNTIL A BROWN, LEATHER-LIKE RING HAS FORMED

→ AROUND TWO MONTHS THERE MAY BE A LIFTING OF THE SCAB AND RUBBING. USE SALVE IF BLOOD APPEARS.

→ BY THREE MONTHS, HAIR SHOULD BE GROWING AROUND AND ON THE AREA WHERE THE HORN PREVIOUSLY WAS LOCATED

DAY ONE. LEATHER RING.

3 MONTHS

CASTRATING

HOW TO

HOW TO CASTRATE A GOAT KID

→ BETWEEN 2-4 MONTHS (NO EARLIER THAN 2!)

→ SEPARATE BUCKLINGS FROM DOELINGS AT 2 MONTHS OF AGE IF YOU CASTRATE LATER

→ PREPARE THE BANDER WITH A BAND

→ SECURE BUCKLING ON HIS SIDE

→ OPEN THE BANDER AS WIDE AS POSSIBLE AND WRAP BAND AROUND THE TESTICLES BUT DO NOT CLOSE IT YET.

→ MAKE SURE THAT BOTH TESTICLES ARE THERE AND THAT THE BAND IS ABOVE THEM

→ CLOSE THE BANDER AND MAKE SURE THE TWO TEETS ARE NOT INSIDE THE BAND

→ ROLL THE BANDS OFF THE BANDER AND DOUBLE CHECK EVERYTHING LOOKS GOOD

BANDER WITH BAND

BANDER AROUND TESTICLES

BUCKLING ON SIDE

CHECKING PLACEMENT

SICK GOAT SYMPTOMS

SEE

→ NOT EATING

→ NOT DRINKING

→ NOT GETTING UP

→ NOT CHEWING CUD

→ NOT URINATING (STRAINING TO URINATE)

→ GOAT POOP NOT PELLETED

→ PALE EYELIDS & GUMS

→ LIMPING OR STAGGERING

→ DROOPING EARS

→ PRESSED HEAD AGAINST FENCE OR WALL

→ BLOATED

→ KICKING BELLY

→ RUNNING NOSE OR EYES

→ ISOLATION

→ HANGING TAIL

→ STANDING HUNCHED

→ DULL COAT

→ SHAKING HEAD

→ SHIVERING

TOUCH

→ HOT UDDER

→ ABNORMAL TEMPERATURE

HEAR

→ GRINDING TEETH

→ COUGHING

→ ABNORMAL CRYING

→ NO RUMEN MOVEMENTS

→ ABNORMAL PANTING OR GROANING

SMELL

→ RECOGNIZE OFF SMELLING GOAT BREATH

→ SWEET OR OFF SMELLING URINE

TASTE

→ BE AWARE OF OFF-TASTING MILK

ALWAYS USE YOUR 5 SENSES WHEN AROUND YOUR GOATS! WATCH FOR ANY OF THESE PROBLEMS AND ACT QUICKLY!

SYMPTOM CHECKER

CHECK EYELIDS

PALE OR WHITE

↓

ANEMIA

↓

BEGIN ANEMIA TREATMENT IMMEDIATELY!

CHECK TEMPERATURE

HIGH TEMP → INFECTION

LOW TEMP

RUMEN ISSUES

LONG-TERM ILLNESS

SIGN THAT THE BODY IS SHUTTING DOWN-- ACT IMMEDIATELY!

DETERMINE SOURCE OF PROBLEM

↓

- INCORRECT FEEDING
- TOXICITY
- DEHYDRATION

↓

POSSIBLE PROBLEMS
- BLOAT
- RUMINAL ACIDOSIS
- OVEREATING DISEASE
- URINARY CALCULI
- KETOSIS
- HYPOCALCEMIA ("MILK FEVER")

WORM & BEGIN ANEMIA TREATMENT IF EYELIDS ARE PALE

DETERMINE SOURCE OF INFECTION OR PROBLEM

↓

POSSIBLE CAUSES
- WOUND
- PNEUMONIA
- DEHYDRATION

↓

- CARE FOR WOUND
- BEGIN ANTIBIOTICS
- RE-HYDRATE!

CHECK FECES

- NOT PELLETED
- DIARRHEA
- COLORED

↓

PARASITE LOAD

OR

STRESS

OR

DIET CHANGES

- RE-HYDRATE!!!
- ADMINSTER BANAMINE TO ALLEVIATE ANY PAIN
- ADMINISTER THIAMINE IF OFF FEED
- TREAT SPECIFIC PROBLEM

- REMOVE TOXIC PLANTS
- KEEP GRAIN STORED PROPERLY
- MAKE ALL FEED CHANGES SLOWLY

MEDICATION KIT: KIDS

MEDICATIONS FOR KIDS

 ALBON

PREVENTS AND TREATS COCCIDIOSIS
 DOSAGE
 GIVE ORALLY, UNDILUTED: 3-5 CC FOR 5 CONSECUTIVE DAYS.

BANAMINE

FEVERISH NEWBORN KID
 DOSAGE
 INJECTION OF NO MORE THAN 1/10 CC IM

COLOSTRUM REPLACERS

SAVE & FREEZE COLOSTRUM FROM DOES WHO HAVE KIDDED ON YOUR PROPERTY. THIS WILL GIVE THE NEWBORN'S THE ANTIBODIES THAT PROVIDE IMMUNITY TO THE ORGANISMS LIVING IN YOUR AREA. IF NO LOCAL COLOSTRUM REPLACER IS AVAILABLE, COMMERCIALLY PREPARED GOAT COLOSTRUM CAN BE USED OR THE RECIPE INCLUDED IN THIS BINDER.
THIS WILL BE BE USED IN THE FIRST 48 HOURS BUT NOT BEYOND THAT.

DOPRAM V

VET PRESCRIPTION. ELIMINATES RESPIRATORY DISTRESS IN NEWBORNS CAUSED BY TROUBLED BIRTHS, INCLUDING C-SECTIONS AND IF KIDS WERE PULLED. KEEP REFRIGERATED.
 DOSAGE
 DROP 2/10 CC UNDER THE KID'S TONGUE IMMEDIATELY UPON BIRTH TO STIMULATE LUNG ACTIVITY.

MOLASSES/KARO SYRUP

USE ORALLY WITH KIDS & ADULT GOATS WHEN QUICK ENERGY IS NEEDED.

PEPTO BISMOL (PINK BISMUTH)

OVER-THE-COUNTER PRODUCT. HELPS WITH IRRITATION/DISTRESS CAUSED BY DIARRHEA IN BOTH KIDS & ADULTS. DETERMINE CAUSE OF DIARRHEA FIRST!
 DOSAGE
 USE UP TO 2 CC EVERY FOUR TO SIX HOURS FOR NEWBORNS;
 5 CC FOR KIDS APPROACHING ONE MONTH OLD & BEYOND.

SPECTUM SCOUR HALT

OVER-THE-COUNTER PRODUCT. IT IS A SULFA-BASED ANTIBIOTIC PRODUCT TO CONTROL DIARRHEA IN KIDS. USAGE WITH ADULT GOATS MAY STOP THE PERISTALTIC ACTION OF THE GUT. FOLLOW LABEL DIRECTIONS WHEN DOSING THE PINKISH-RED LIQUID INTO THE GOAT'S MOUTH.

MEDICATION KIT: SICKNESS & INJURY

MEDICATIONS FOR SICKNESS & INJURY

ACTIVATED CHARCOAL

ACTIVATED CHARCOAL ABSORBS TOXINS IN A GOAT AND CAN BE USED IN CASES OF TOXICITY. MIX ONE TABLESPOON CHARCOAL WITH A BIT OF WATER. IT NEEDS TO LOOK LIKE A SLURRY. SYRINGE IT INTO THE GOAT. FOLLOW AN HOUR LATER WITH MILK OF MAGNESIA. THE DOSE FOR M.O.M. IS 15 CC PER 60 LBS.

BANAMINE

VET PRESCRIPTION REQUIRED. KEEP REFRIGERATED. MUST-HAVE MEDICATION; NEVER RUN OUT. ANTI-INFLAMMATORY, HELPS TO REDUCE FEVER, SOOTHES IRRITATION IN THE GASTRO INTESTINAL TRACT (GUT) WHEN DIARRHEA OR OTHER GUT-RELATED DIGESTIVE ILLNESSES OCCUR. RELIEVES PAIN AND SORENESS ASSOCIATED WITH ANIMAL BITES AND OTHER INJURIES. USE NO MORE FREQUENTLY THAN EVERY 12 HOURS (STOMACH ULCERS ARE POSSIBLE.)

DOSAGE
1 CC PER 100 LBS BODY WEIGHT IM

DRAXXIN

VET PRESCRIPTION. INJECTABLE RESPIRATORY ANTIBIOTIC. VERY EXPENSIVE PRODUCT THAT PURPORTS TO BE A ONE-TIME-ONLY USAGE ANTIBIOTIC. BECAUSE GOATS HAVE THE FASTEST METABOLISM OF ALL RUMINANTS, THEY NEED TO BE DOSED DAILY FOR FIVE DAYS.

DOSAGE
1.1 CC/100 LBS

DYNE

OVER-THE-COUNTER ORAL HIGH-CALORIE FOOD SUPPLEMENT. USE FOR ANIMALS OFF FEED OR NEEDING QUICK ENERGY. MUST HAVE PRODUCT.

DOSAGE
1 OZ. PER ANIMAL, THREE (3) TIMES PER DAY.

ELECTROLYTES

OVER-THE-COUNTER PRODUCTS PACKAGED IN POWDERED FORM. REHYDRATES SICK ANIMALS. STORE IN A COOL, DRY PLACE. NEVER BE WITHOUT THIS PRODUCT! OR USE THE RECIPE INCLUDED IN THIS BINDER.

USAGE
* *USE AS AN ORAL DRENCH*
* *PUT INTO BABY BOTTLES FOR KIDS TO SUCK*
* *OR MIX IN DRINKING WATER*

MEDICATION KIT: SICKNESS & INJURY

MEDICATIONS FOR SICKNESS & INJURY

→ FORTIFIED VITAMIN B COMPLEX

OVER-THE-COUNTER PRODUCT. MUST BE FORTIFIED OR THE DOSAGE NEEDS TO BE MULTIPLIED BY 4. THIS FORTIFIED VITAMIN IS WATER SOLUBLE.

DOSAGE
4 CC PER 100 POUNDS BODY WEIGHT

→ GOAT NUTRIDRENCH

ORAL QUICK ENERGY SUPPLEMENT. GIVE TO STRESSED AND/OR OFF-FEED GOATS. CONTAINS MANY OF THE VITAMINS, MINERALS, AND NUTRIENTS THAT A SICK GOAT REQUIRES TO SURVIVE ITS ILLNESS.

→ MILK OF MAGNESIA

AN OVER-THE-COUNTER LAXATIVE PRODUCT USED FOR CONSTIPATION AND TOXICITY REACTIONS (TO MOVE TOXIC MATERIALS FROM THE BODY). IT CAN BE USED TO TREAT BLOAT, RUMINAL ACIDOSIS, OVEREATING DISEASE, AND FLOPPY KID SYNDROME.

DOSAGE
ORAL DRENCH AT A RATE OF 15 CC PER 60 LBS BODY WEIGHT EVERY FOUR TO SIX HOURS. THE FECES SHOULD GO FROM NORMAL TO CLUMPY THEN BACK TO NORMAL "PILLS". ALWAYS KEEP THE ANIMAL HYDRATED WITH ELECTROLYTES WHEN USING MILK OF MAGNESIA OR OTHER LAXATIVES.

→ NUFLOR GOLD (FLORFENICOL)

VET PRESCRIPTION. GREAT ANTIBIOTIC FOR RESPIRATORY PROBLEMS, INCLUDING PNEUMONIA. CAN ALSO BE USED TO TRY TO KEEP MASTITIS FROM BECOMING SYSTEMIC. THIS LIQUID IS THICK! USE LUER LOCK SYRINGES BECAUSE THE NEEDLE MAY BLOW OFF THE SYRINGE. KEEP REFRIGERATED.

DOSAGE
6 CC PER 100 LBS BODYWEIGHT GIVEN IM FOR FIVE CONSECUTIVE DAYS. NEWBORN KIDS SHOULD RECEIVE NO LESS THAN 1/2 CC.

→ PENICILLIN, PROCAINE (3000,000 IU)

OVER-THE-COUNTER PRODUCT. USED FOR TREATMENT OF LISTERIOSIS, GOAT POLIO, INJURIES, BITES, AND DIFFICULT BIRTHS. KEEP REFRIGERATED. KEEP ON HAND!

DOSAGE
1 CC/20 LBS SQ INJECTION FOR 5 DAYS
NOTES: USE A 16 OR 18 GAUGE NEEDLE

MEDICATION KIT: SICKNESS & INJURY

PEPTO BISMOL (PINK BISMUTH)
*OVER-THE-COUNTER PRODUCT. HELPS WITH IRRITATION/DISTRESS CAUSED BY DIARRHEA IN BOTH KIDS AND ADULTS. **DETERMINE CAUSE OF DIARRHEA FIRST!***

DOSAGE
USE AS MUCH AS 10-15 CC FOR ADULTS

PIRSUE
VET PRESCRIPTION MASTITIS MEDICATION. EXPENSIVE BUT EXCELLENT PRODUCT.

PROBIOTICS (PROBIOS)
OVER-THE-COUNTER ORAL RUMINANT GEL.
***USE AFTER:** ANTIOBIOTIC THERAPY, TREATMENT FOR DIARRHEA (SCOURS), AND DAILY WHEN GOATS ARE IN SHIPMENT AND TO SETTLE THE STOMACH. KEEP REFRIGERATED.*

RED CELL
OVER-THE-COUNTER PRODUCT. (A FLAVORED ORAL IRON SUPPLEMENT MADE FOR HORSES.)

DOSAGE
4 CC ORALLY DAILY TO TREAT ANEMIA.

THIAMINE (VITAMIN B1)
VET PRESCRIPTION. GIVE TO ANY GOAT THAT IS OFF-FEED. ALSO USED TO TREAT GOAT POLIO AND LISTERIOSIS. KEEP REFRIGERATED.

DOSAGE
4 CC PER 100 POUNDS BODY WEIGHT UP TO THREE TIMES PER DAY IM OR SQ.

VITAMIN B-12
VET PRESCRIPTION. A RED-COLORED INJECTABLE LIQUID. ESSENTIAL FOR USE WITH GOATS WHO ARE ANEMIC FROM WORMS. ALSO AN APPETITE STIMULANT. KEEPS BEST REFRIGERATED.

DOSAGE
ADMINISTER 4 CC PER 100 LBS BODY WEIGHT IM.

MEDICATION KIT: DISEASES/ VACCINATIONS

MEDICATIONS FOR DISEASES & VACCINATIONS

 BOSE

VET PRESCRIPTION. SELENIUM DEFICIENCY (WHITE MUSCLE DISEASE, NUTRITIONAL MUSCULAR DISTROPHY). KNOW YOUR STATE, LOCAL, AND FEED SELENIUM LEVELS BEFORE USING THIS MEDICATION. SELENIUM IS TOXIC AT LOW DOSAGES, AND THE DOSING MARGIN OF SAFETY IS NARROW. IT IS EASY TO OVERDOSE SELENIUM.

DOSAGE
GIVE 1/2 CC IM AT BIRTH, THEN AT 1 MONTH.
PREGNANT DOES: GIVE 2 1/2 CC PER 100 LBS 4-6 WEEKS BEFORE KIDDING.
BUCKS: GIVE 2 1/2 CC PER 100 LBS TWO TIMES A YEAR.

C&D ANTI-TOXIN

MUST HAVE MEDICATION. OVER-THE-COUNTER PRODUCT. ALWAYS HAVE ON HAND. USED FOR BITES, BLOAT, INGESTION OF TOXIC SUBSTANCES, RUMINAL ACIDOSIS, OVEREATING DISEASE, DIARRHEA, AND FLOPPY KID SYNDROME.
SHORT TERM PROTECTION (ABOUT 12 HOURS). MUST BE REFRIGERATED.
WAIT 5 DAYS AFTER ADMINISTERING AND THEN REVACCINATE WITH INITIAL CD/T VACCINE AND A BOOSTER AT 30 DAYS.

CDT VACCINATION

CD/T VACCINE (CLOSTRIDIUM PERFRINGENS TYPES C&D + TETANUS TOXOID VACCINE). OVER-THE-COUNTER VACCINE. PROVIDES PROTECTION AGAINST OVEREATING DISEASE (TYPES C&D AND TETANUS.)

DOSAGE
GIVE SQ. KIDS 1-3 MONTHS-AND ALL NEWLY-PURCHASED ANIMALS (ALL AGES) VACCINATE WITH 2 CC.
GIVE THE SECOND VACCINATION 30 DAYS LATER.
GIVE 2 CC ANNUALLY PER GOAT AFTER THAT.

NOTES
GIVING 2 INJECTIONS, 30 DAYS APART, IS WHAT GIVES THE LONG-TERM PROTECTION.
AN INJECTION-SITE ABCESS MAY APPEAR BUT THIS IS ACTUALLY THE GOAT'S POSITIVE REACTION TO THE VACCINE. AND USUALLY GOES AWAY IN TIME.

QUICK TIP

ORAL DRENCHING: MEDICATIONS SYRINGED INTO A GOAT'S MOUTH AND DOWN THE THROAT

MEDICATION KIT: DISEASES/ VACCINATIONS

MEDICATIONS FOR DISEASES & VACCINATIONS

 PNEUOMONIA VACCINE: PRESPONSE HM & POLY BAC SOMNUS

DOSAGE

1 CC FOR GOATS UNDER 60 LBS

2 CC FOR GOATS OVER 60 LBS

THIS IS A TWO INJECTION SERIES 21 DAYS APART THE FIRST TIME AND ANNUALLY THEREAFTER.

 TETANUS ANTI-TOXIN

OVER-THE-COUNTER PRODUCT. USED FOR IMMEDIATE AND SHORT-TERM PROTECTION AGAINST TETANUS (LOCKJAW) WHEN THE PROBLEM EXISTS. TETANUS IS FATAL IF NOT PROMPTLY TREATED. COMES IN SINGLE-DOSE 1500 UNIT VIALS. KEEP REFRIGERATED.

DOSAGE

USE THE ENTIRE 1500 UNIT VIAL IM FOR ADULTS.

USE HALF THE 1500 UNIT VIAL FOR KIDS.

NO SOONER THAN FIVE DAYS AFTER THIS MEDICATION IS LAST USED, YOU MUST REVACCINATE WITH TETANUS TOXOID OR CD/T (THE COMPLETE TWO-INJECTION SERIES GIVEN 30 DAYS APART) TO REINSTATE LONG-TERM PROTECTION.

QUICK TIP

SQ = SUBCUTANEOUSLY=
SHOT GIVEN UNDER THE SKIN

IM = INTRAMUSCULAR=
SHOT GIVEN INTO THE MUSCLE

MEDICATION KIT: WORMS

MEDICATIONS FOR WORMS

 ALBON

PREVENTS AND TREATS COCCIDIOSIS. GIVE ORALLY, UNDILUTED.

> **DOSAGE**
> *5-10 CC FOR FIVE CONSECUTIVE DAYS*

IVOMEC 1% INJECTABLE (IVERMECTIN)

OVER-THE-COUNTER PRODUCT. USED FOR ELIMINATING STOMACH WORMS. STORE IN COOL TEMPERATURES AND KEEP OUT OF SUNLIGHT. ACHIEVES A QUICKER "KILL" VIA ORAL DOSING. ALSO USED IN TREATMENT OF MENINGEAL DEERWORM INFECTION. CLEAR DEWORMERS DO NOT KILL TAPEWORMS. IVERMECTIN 1% IS ONE OF SEVERAL DEWORMERS USED TO KILL STOMACH WORMS.

> **DOSAGE**
> *THIS CLEAR LIQUID WORKS BEST IF USED ORALLY AT A RATE OF 1 CC PER 35 POUNDS BODY WEIGHT. DO NOT UNDER-DOSE.*

SAFEGUARD (PANACUR)

WHITE-COLORED DEWORMER. NO LONGER KILLS STOMACH WORMS IN MOST OF USA. USED TO KILL TAPEWORMS AND MENINGEAL DEERWORM INFECTION.

> **DOSAGE**
> *1 CC PER 10 LBS GIVEN ORALLY*

SPECTUM SCOUR HALT

OVER-THE-COUNTER PRODUCT. IT IS A SULFA-BASED ANTIBIOTIC PRODUCT TO CONTROL DIARRHEA IN KIDS. USAGE WITH ADULT GOATS MAY STOP THE PERISTALTIC ACTION OF THE GUT.

> **DOSAGE**
> *FOLLOW LABEL DIRECTIONS WHEN DOSING THE PINKISH-RED LIQUID INTO THE GOAT'S MOUTH. 1 CC PER 10 POUNDS.*

SULMET OR DI-METHOX 12.5%

TREATS COCCIDIOSIS

> **DOSAGE**
> *GIVE ORALLY FOR 5 DAYS WITH A DOSE OF 1 CC PER 5 LBS ON THE FIRST DAY AND 1 CC PER 10 LBS ON DAYS 2-5.*

HOW TO EXAMINE FOR ANEMIA:

1. PUT THUMB ON EYELID AND CLOSE EYELID OVER EYEBALL.
2. PUSH DOWN ON THE EYEBALL. YOU SHOULD SEE THE EYELASHES OF THE UPPER EYELID CURLING OVER YOUR THUMB.
3. PULL DOWN THE LOWER EYELID.
4. THE MUCOUS MEMBRANES WILL POP INTO VIEW.
5. MATCH THE COLOR OF THE PINKEST PORTION OF THE MUCOUS MEMBRANES TO THE COLORS ON THIS CHART.

A(1)

B(2)

ANEMIA GUIDE
COLOR BASED ON THE FAMACHA AMENIA GUIDE

C(3)

BORDERLINE

WATCH, POSSIBLY DEWORM & POSSIBLY BEGIN ANEMIA TREATMENT

D(4)

DANGEROUS!

DEWORM & BEGIN ANEMIA TREATMENT IMMEDIATELY!

E(5)

FATAL

DEWORM & BEGIN ANEMIA TREATMENT IMMEDIATELY!!!

ANEMIA TREATMENT PLAN

ANEMIA TREATMENT PLAN

WEEKLY CHECK EYELIDS AND COMPARE TO SCORE CARD. IF ANEMIC...

1. De-Worm
2. Check Goat's Coat for External Blood Sucking Parasites
3. Administer B Vitamins
4. Give Iron Supplements
5. Provide Exceptional Nutritional Support
6. Re-Evaluate in 2 Weeks

WORM

ADMINISTER WORMER, AND GIVE AGAIN IN 10 DAYS TO CATCH THE WORMS THAT HATCHED WITHIN THAT TIME FRAME.

IVOMEC 1% INJECTABLE (IVERMECTIN)

DOSAGE

THIS CLEAR LIQUID WORKS BEST IF USED ORALLY AT A RATE OF 1 CC PER 35 POUNDS BODY WEIGHT. DO NOT UNDER-DOSE.

FORTIFIED VITAMIN B COMPLEX (OR B-12)

GIVE DAILY INJECTIONS FOR UP TO 2 WEEKS.

DOSAGE:

GIVE 4 CC/100 LBS, SQ

RED CELL

RED CELL IS AN IRON SUPPLEMENT THAT CAN BE GIVEN DAILY FOR UP TO 2 WEEKS OR UNTIL THE GOAT'S FAMACHA SCORE IS ACCEPTABLE.

DOSAGE:

4 CC DAILY, ORALLY

NUTRITIONAL SUPPORT

FEED HIGH QUALITY HAY DURING THIS TIME. GIVE YOUR GOAT NUTRI-DRENCH THE FIRST 5 DAYS OF TREATING ANEMIA. PROVIDE MOLASSES WATER AND ELECTROLYTES IF GOAT IS OFF FEED AND NOT DRINKING. CONSIDER GIVING YOUR GOAT A COPPER BOLUS BECAUSE COPPER WILL SUPPORT YOUR GOAT'S ABILITY TO KEEP PARASITES AT BAY.

RE-EVALUATE

HOPEFULLY BY THIS TIME YOU HAVE SEEN A MARKED DIFFERENCE IN YOUR GOAT. IF NOT, CONTINUE THIS TREATMENT UNTIL THE RESULTS ARE ADEQUATE. CONSULT YOUR VET IF YOU HAVE ANY MORE CONCERNS OR QUESTIONS.

PNEUMONIA TREATMENT PLAN

PNEUMONIA TREATMENT PLAN

ACT QUICKLY. PNEUMONIA CAN KILL A GOAT IN AS LITTLE AS 4 HOURS.

1. Bring down the temperature immediately & alleviate pain
2. Give antibiotic
3. Relieve chest congestion if needed
4. Give electrolytes to a dehydrated goat
5. Give thiamine to a goat off feed
6. Give probiotics to any goat that has been on antibiotics
7. Consider vaccinating

 BANAMINE

THE HIGH TEMPERATURE MUST BE BROUGHT DOWN IMMEDIATELY. THIS WILL ALSO ALLEVIATE ANY PAIN AND INFLAMMATION THEY ARE EXPERIENCING.

DOSAGE
1 CC PER 100 POUNDS. NEWBORNS/YOUNG KIDS: ONE-TENTH TO TWO-TENTHS OF A CC. (IM)

 ANTIBIOTIC: NUFLOR, NUFLOR GOLD, EXCENEL RTU, DRAXXIN OR PENICILLIN

NUFLOR: 18-GUAGE NEEDLE WITH A LUER-LOCK SYRINGE.
3 CC PER 100 POUNDS OF BODY WEIGHT (IM) FOR 5 CONSECUTIVE DAYS.

NUFLOR GOLD: 18-GUAGE NEEDLE WITH A LUER-LOCK SYRINGE.
6 CC PER 100 POUNDS BODY WEIGHT (IM) FOR 5 CONSECUTIVE DAYS. PROVIDES SOME PROTECTION AGAINST MYCOPLASMA THAT NUFLOR DOESN'T HAVE.
NEWBORN KIDS: MINIMUM DOSAGE OF 1/2 CC.

EXCENEL RT: 18-GUAGE NEEDLE.
3 CC PER 100 POUNDS BODY WEIGHT (IM) FOR 5 CONSECUTIVE DAYS. THE SECOND DOSE IS GIVEN 12 HOURS AFTER THE FIRST AND THE NEXT FOUR DOSES GIVEN 24 HOURS AFTER THE LAST. NEWBORNS/YOUNG KIDS: GREAT OPTION. MINIMUM DOSAGE FOR NEWBORNS IS 1/2 CC.

DRAXXIN: POSSIBLY MORE EXPENSIVE THAN OTHER ALTERNATIVES BUT VERY EFFECTIVE.
I CC PER 100 POUNDS BODY WEIGHT (IM) FOR 5 CONSECUTIVE DAYS.

PENICILLIN: 18-GAUGE NEEDLE.
5 CC PER 100 POUNDS BODY WEIGHT (SQ OVER RIBS) FOR 5 CONSECUTIVE DAYS.

LA200: 18 GAUGE NEEDLE.
5 CC PER 100 POUNDS BODY WEIGHT (SQ OVER RIBS) FOR 5 CONSECUTIVE DAYS.

ALWAYS HAVE **EPINEPHRINE ON HAND WHEN GIVING INJECTIONS JUST IN CASE OF ANAPHYLACTIC SHOCK*

PNEUMONIA TREATMENT PLAN

PNEUMONIA TREATMENT PLAN

→ ROBITUSSIN DM

ONLY IF PRESENT, CHEST CONGESTION CAN BE RELIEVED BY GIVING ROBITUSSIN DM.

DOSAGE

TWICE DAILY AT A DOSAGE OF APPROXIMATELY 6 CC PER 100 POUNDS BODY WEIGHT.

→ ELECTROLYTES

IF THE GOAT IS DEHYDRATED, REPLENISH FLUIDS WITH ELECTROLYTES BY ORALLY DRENCHING THE GOAT. IN A 24 HOUR PERIOD, A 100 POUND GOAT NEEDS 1 GALLON OF FLUIDS. THIS WILL BE GIVEN IN SMALL AMOUNTS THROUGHOUT THE DAY. BUT GREAT CARE MUST BE TAKEN SO THAT THE GOAT DOES NOT ASPIRATE THE FLUIDS INTO ITS LUNGS.

→ THIAMINE

THIAMINE MUST BE GIVEN IF THE GOAT IS OFF FEED. THEIR BRAIN FUNCTION DEPENDS ON IT AND THEIR RUMENS PRODUCE IT, BUT WILL STOP PRODUCING IT IF THEY ARE OFF FEED.

DOSAGE

4 CC PER 100 POUNDS BODY WEIGHT (IM OR SQ EVERY 12 HOURS).

→ PROBIOTICS

AFTER ANY ROUND OF ANTIBIOTICS, REPLENISH A GOAT WITH PROBIOTICS.

→ VACCINATE

CONSIDER VACCINATING YOUR HERD IF PNEUMONIA IS A PROBLEM. PRESPONSE HM PNEUMONIA VACCINE BY BERINGER INGLEHEIM. JEFFERS CARRIES THIS OVER THE COUNTER FROM JEFFERS LIVESTOCK.

DOSAGE

1 CC SQ FOR GOATS UNDER 60 POUNDS AND 2 CC FOR GOATS OVER 60 POUNDS. REPEAT DOSAGE 4 WEEKS LATER. AND THEN ANNUALLY AFTER THAT.

SYMPTOMS OF PNEUMONIA

1. *HIGH FEVER (104°-106°F)*
2. *LOW TEMPERATURE (AFTER HIGH TEMPERATURE IT FALLS BELOW 100°F)*
3. *NOT EATING*
4. *STANDING OFF BY ITSELF*
5. *TAIL AND HEAD DOWN*
6. *LAY DOWN, MOAN, AND GET UP BECAUSE OF PAIN (FLUID FILLING LUNGS)*
7. *DOWN AND UNABLE TO GET UP (FLUID-FILLED LUNGS)*
8. *NASAL DISCHARGE*
9. *DIFFICULTY BREATHING*
10. *MOIST, PAINFUL COUGH*
11. *DEPRESSION*

MEDICATIONS A-Z FOR SICKNESS & INJURY

A-180 (DANOFLOXACIN)
VET PRESCRIPTION. INJECTABLE RESPIRATORY ANTIBIOTIC. NOT RECOMMENDED.

ALBADRY PLUS
TEAT INFUSION MEDICATION CONTAINING PROCAINE PENICILLIN AND NOVOBIOCIN SODIUM FOR TREATING MASTITIS IN NON-LACTATING GOATS AND DRYING UP LACTATING GOATS. CAN BE USED TOPICALLY ON STAPH INFECTIONS. BEST TO HAVE THE UDDER'S CONTENTS TESTED TO FIND OUT WHICH ORGANISM IS CAUSING THE INFECTION SO YOU CAN CHOOSE THE BEST ANTIBIOTIC.

ALBON (SULFADIMETHOXINE 12.5% OR ITS GENERIC EQUIVALENT DIMETHOX 12.5%)
THESE PRODUCTS ARE THE DRUG OF CHOICE FOR PREVENTING AND TREATING COCCIDIOSIS.

DOSAGE
GIVE ORALLY UNDILUTED TO KIDS AT A RATE OF 3-5 CC AND TO ADULTS AT A RATE OF 5-10 CC FOR FIVE CONSECUTIVE DAYS. MIXING WITH DRINKING WATER AS DIRECTED ON THE LABEL IS ANOTHER OPTION, BUT NOT RECOMMENDED. SICK GOATS SHOULD BE TREATED INDIVIDUALLY WITH ORAL DOSING FOR FIVE CONSECUTIVE DAYS. THE GALLON JUG IS THE MOST COST-EFFECTIVE PURCHASE. WILL NOT WORK WITH AUTOMATIC WATERERS DUE TO CONTINUAL DILUTION OF THE PRODUCT.

ALBON 40% INJECTABLE
OVER-THE-COUNTER AND DOSED ORALLY TO TREAT COCCIDIOSIS.

DOSAGE
1.56 CC GIVEN ORALLY ON FIRST DAY PER 25 POUNDS BODYWEIGHT; DAYS 2-5, DOSE AT .78 CC PER 25 POUNDS BODYWEIGHT. MIX WITH NUTRI-DRENCH OR SIMILAR PRODUCT FOR PALATABILITY.

ALUSHIELD
ALUMINUM-BASED WATER-RESISTANT AEROSOL BANDAGE FOR TOPICAL USE ONLY.

BANAMINE (FLUMEGLUMINE)
VET PRESCRIPTION REQUIRED. ANTI-INFLAMMATORY THAT HELPS REDUCE FEVER, SOOTHES IRRITATION IN THE GASTRO-INTESTINAL TRACT (GUT) WHEN DIARRHEA OR OTHER GUT-RELATED DIGESTIVE ILLNESSES OCCUR, RELIEVES PAIN AND SORENESS ASSOCIATED WITH ANIMAL BITES AND OTHER INJURIES. USE NO MORE FREQUENTLY THAN EVERY 12 HOURS (STOMACH ULCERS ARE POSSIBLE) UNLESS GOAT IS DYING, JUSTIFYING THE RISK. KEEPS BEST IN HOT CLIMATES WHEN REFRIGERATED. MUST-HAVE MEDICATION; NEVER RUN OUT.

DOSAGE
1 CC PER 100 LBS. BODY WEIGHT IM. A NEWBORN KID WITH A FEVER CAN RECEIVE AN INJECTION OF NO MORE THAN 1/10 CC IM.

MEDICATIONS: A-Z

MEDICATIONS A-Z FOR SICKNESS & INJURY

 BAYTRIL 100 (ENROFLOXACIN 100 MG/ML)

VET PRESCRIPTION. (NOT BAYTRIL 2.27%). USAGE IN GOATS IS "OFF-LABEL" OR "EXTRA-LABEL," BUT THIS ANTIBIOTIC IS BEING USED IN GOATS BY SOME VETERINARIANS.

THIS MEDICATION IS VERY EFFECTIVE AGAINST GUT-RELATED ILLNESSES AND WORKS SYNERGISTICALLY (BETTER TOGETHER THAN INDIVIDUALLY) WITH SMZ (SULFADIMETHOXAZINE WITH TRIMETHOPRIM). SOME JURISDICTIONS PROHIBIT USE OF BAYTRIL OR BAYTRIL 100 IN ANY FORM (INJECTABLE OR TABLETS) IN FOOD-PRODUCTION ANIMALS BECAUSE THE WITHDRAWAL TIME FROM MEAT AND MILK HAS NOT BEEN DETERMINED. GREAT FOR TREATING JOINT ILL WHEN NO OTHER ANTIBIOTIC WORKS. IF YOU HAVE A SICK GOAT ON WHICH NO OTHER ANTIBIOTIC IS WORKING, BAYTRIL 100 IS THE DRUG OF LAST RESORT. DO NOT USE WITHOUT VET APPROVAL AND SUPERVISION.

DOSAGE
4 CC'S PER 100 LBS. OF BODY WEIGHT FOR FIVE CONSECUTIVE DAYS.

 BEET PULP, SHREDDED

ALTHOUGH NOT A MEDICATION, IT IS USEFUL AND OFTEN MISUSED. SHREDDED BEET PULP ADDS FIBER TO THE RUMEN OF OLD GOATS WHOSE TEETH HAVE BEGUN TO WEAR. THIS IS IN ADDITION TO THEIR NORMAL FEED, NOT IN PLACE OF IT.

 BIOSOL (NEOMYCIN SULFATE)

OVER-THE-COUNTER SULFA-BASED ANTIBIOTIC FOR USING WITH SCOURING KIDS AND ADULTS WHEN COCCIDIOSIS IS NOT THE UNDERLYING ILLNESS. WORKS EFFECTIVELY AGAINST E.COLI AND OTHER DIGESTIVE-SYSTEM BACTERIAL INFECTIONS. DO NOT OVERDOSE; CONSTIPATION CAN RESULT. DO NOT STOP DIARRHEA UNTIL YOU KNOW ITS CAUSE. SOMETIMES DIARRHEA IS THE BODY'S WAY OF ELIMINATING TOXINS.

DOSAGE
FOR KIDS, GIVE 3 CC ORALLY EVERY 12 HOURS UNTIL DIARRHEA HAS STOPPED AND FECES IS NORMAL. FOR ADULT GOATS, USE 5 CC TO 10 CC ORALLY AND AS DIRECTED FOR USAGE IN KIDS.

BLACK OIL SUNFLOWER SEEDS (BOSS)

ANOTHER NON-MEDICATION, IT IS USEFUL TO ADD FAT TO THE DIET OF THIN AND/OR OLD GOATS. BOSS IS 25% FAT.

QUICK TIP

If a goat has diarrhea, always find out WHY they have diarrhea first, then treat the problem.

MEDICATIONS: A-Z

MEDICATIONS A-Z FOR SICKNESS & INJURY

 ### BOSE (NOT MUSE)

VET PRESCRIPTION. (MUSE IS A HORSE PRODUCT AND IS TOO STRONG & SHOULD NOT BE USED WITH GOATS.) INJECTABLE MEDICATION FOR SELENIUM DEFICIENCY (WHITE MUSCLE DISEASE, AKA NUTRITIONAL MUSCULAR DISTROPHY). SELENIUM DEFICIENCY EXISTS AT DIFFERENT LEVELS THROUGHOUT THE UNITED STATES. IT IS CRITICAL TO FOLLOW YOUR VETERINARIAN'S DIRECTIONS ON THE USAGE OF THESE PRODUCTS, AS WELL AS OFFERING SUPPLEMENTAL LOOSE MINERALS CONTAINING SELENIUM. GOOGLE "SELENIUM DEFICIENCY" TO SEE THE GENERAL LOCATIONS IN THE USA. MOST OF THE EAST COAST, DOWN TO FLORIDA AND WESTWARD THROUGH THE GREAT LAKES REGION, PLUS THE WEST COAST, INCLUDING CALIFORNIA AND PARTS OF NEVADA AND IDAHO, ARE SELENIUM DEFICIENT TO DIFFERENT DEGREES. SELENIUM DEFICIENCY USUALLY SHOWS ITSELF IN THE FORM OF WEAK REAR LEGS IN KIDS. OLDER GOATS DON'T PUT ON WEIGHT, HAVE WEAK LEGS, AND GENERALLY STAY IN POOR CONDITION AND POOR HEALTH. SELENIUM IS TOXIC AT LOW DOSAGES, AND THE DOSING MARGIN OF SAFETY IS NARROW. THE ADDITION OF SELENIUM TO FEED IS CONTROLLED BY US LAW. IN SOME AREAS, PRODUCERS ONLY NEED TO PROVIDE LOOSE MINERALS CONTAINING SELENIUM. IN OTHER REGIONS, SELENIUM INJECTIONS ARE NECESSARY.
IT IS EASY TO OVERDOSE SELENIUM.

DOSAGE

WHEN BOSE INJECTIONS ARE REQUIRED, THEY ARE USUALLY GIVEN AT BIRTH AND AGAIN AT ONE MONTH OF AGE (1/2 CC IM). PREGNANT DOES RECEIVE INJECTIONS FOUR TO SIX WEEKS BEFORE KIDDING, AND BUCKS ARE VACCINATED TWICE A YEAR. ADULT DOSAGE OF BOSE IS 2-1/2 CC PER 100 LBS BODYWEIGHT GIVEN IM.

 ### C&D ANTI-TOXIN

OVER-THE-COUNTER MADE-FOR-GOATS PRODUCT THAT CAN BE SAFELY USED FOR MANY PROBLEMS WHEN THEY ALREADY EXIST LIKE: SEVERE DIARRHEA IN VERY YOUNG KIDS, TOXICITY CAUSED BY PLANTS, POISONS (BITES, OVEREATING DISEASE, BLOAT, RUMINAL ACIDOSIS, AND INGESTION OF TOXIC SUBSTANCES LIKE AZALEAS AND ANTIFREEZE ARE SEVERAL EXAMPLES). THIS IS ONE OF THE PRODUCTS ADMINISTERED TO COMBAT FLOPPY KID SYNDROME. C&D ANTI-TOXIN PROVIDES SHORT-TERM PROTECTION (ABOUT 12 HOURS) BUT WORKS QUICKLY TOWARDS SOLVING THE IMMEDIATE PROBLEM. MUST BE REFRIGERATED. FREEZES AT VERY HIGH TEMPERATURES. C&D ANTI-TOXIN NEGATES ANY PROTECTION PREVIOUSLY GIVEN BY THE CD/T VACCINE, SO YOU MUST WAIT FOR AT LEAST FIVE DAYS AFTER COMPLETION OF C&D ANTI-TOXIN THERAPY AND RE-VACCINATE THE ANIMAL WITH THE INITIAL CD/T VACCINE INJECTION PLUS THE BOOSTER 30 DAYS THEREAFTER. MUST-HAVE MEDICATION. ALWAYS HAVE ON HAND. THERE IS NO SUBSTITUTE.

DOSAGE
FOLLOW LABEL DIRECTIONS.

MEDICATIONS A-Z FOR SICKNESS & INJURY

➜ CD/T VACCINE (CLOSTRIDIUM PERFRINGENS TYPES C&D + TETANUS TOXOID VACCINE)

CD/T VACCINE (CLOSTRIDIUM PERFRINGENS TYPES C&D + TETANUS TOXOID VACCINE) - OVER-THE-COUNTER MADE-FOR-GOATS PRODUCT THAT PROVIDES LONG-TERM PROTECTION AGAINST OVEREATING DISEASE (TYPES C&D) AND TETANUS. IT MAY CAUSE AN INJECTION-SITE ABSCESS, WHICH IS AN INDICATION OF THE BODY'S POSITIVE REACTION TO THE VACCINE. IN MOST CASES, THE ABSCESS GOES AWAY IN TIME.

DOSAGE

KIDS OF ONE TO THREE MONTHS OF AGE AND ALL NEWLY-PURCHASED ANIMALS REGARDLESS OF AGE SHOULD BE VACCINATED WITH 2 CC AND THEN A SECOND VACCINATION SHOULD BE GIVEN 30 DAYS LATER. TWO INJECTIONS 30 DAYS APART ARE REQUIRED IN ORDER TO PROVIDE LONG-TERM PROTECTION. ANNUALLY THEREAFTER, ONE INJECTION OF 2 CC PER GOAT WILL RENEW THE PROTECTION. GIVE SQ.

➜ CASEOUS LYMPHADENITIS (CL) VACCINE

INTRODUCED IN MAY 2012 BY TEXAS VET LAB OF SAN ANGELO, TEXAS. OVER THE COUNTER IN SOME STATES; PRESCRIPTION ITEM IN OTHER STATES. NOT AVAILABLE YET IN A FEW STATES. JEFFERS CAN TELL YOU WHAT EACH STATE REQUIRES.
CALL 1-800-533-3377 AND ASK TO SPEAK WITH THEIR CL VACCINE EXPERT.

➜ CHONDROPROTEC

A SKIN REGROWING MEDICATION. APPLIED TOPICALLY. VET PRESCRIPTION.

➜ COLOSTRUM REPLACERS & SUPPLEMENTS

DO NOT CONFUSE THESE TWO TYPES OF PRODUCTS. NEWBORNS MUST HAVE COLOSTRUM DURING THE FIRST HOURS AFTER BIRTH. IF THE DAM IS COLOSTRUM DEFICIENT, YOU MUST USE A COLOSTRUM REPLACER. THE BEST COLOSTRUM REPLACER IS COLOSTRUM SAVED (AND FROZEN) FROM DOES ON YOUR PROPERTY WHO HAVE ALREADY KIDDED. THIS COLOSTRUM WILL HAVE ANTIBODIES THAT PROVIDE THE KIDS NEEDED IMMUNITY TO THE ORGANISMS EXISTING IN YOUR PARTICULAR LOCATION. IF YOU DON'T HAVE A SUPPLY OF FROZEN COLOSTRUM, THEN YOU MUST USE A COMMERCIALLY-PREPARED GOAT COLOSTRUM REPLACER (*NOT* "SUPPLEMENT"). DO NOT USE COLOSTRUM OR COLOSTRUM REPLACER BEYOND THE FIRST 48 HOURS OF THE KID'S LIFE. SWITCH TO GOAT MILK OR GOAT MILK REPLACER. COLOSTRUM HAS ALREADY DONE ITS JOB FOR THE NEWBORN AFTER 48 HOURS AND THE KID'S BODY CAN BETTER DIGEST GOAT MILK. ULTRA-BAC 24 ALL-SPECIES MILK REPLACER (MILK PRODUCTS) IS A GOOD OPTION.

QUICK TIP

Any time you are around your goats, use your 5 senses. Observe and quickly treat any sickness you observe!

MEDICATIONS: A-Z

MEDICATIONS A-Z FOR SICKNESS & INJURY

CORID (AMPROLLIUM)

OVER-THE-COUNTER PRODUCT FOR PREVENTING AND TREATING COCCIDIOSIS. COMES IN GRANULAR PACKETS AND GALLON LIQUID. **THIS PRODUCT IS A THIAMINE INHIBITOR,** *KNOWLEDGEABLE PROFESSIONALS RECOMMEND AGAINST ITS USE. ALBON OR ITS GENERIC EQUIVALENT SULFADIMETHOXINE 12.5% (DIMETHOX 12.5%) IS PREFERRED OVER CORID. IF YOU MUST USE CORID, BUY THE GALLON LIQUID AND MAINTAIN BETTER CONTROL OVER DOSAGES.*

DOSAGE

FOLLOW PACKAGE DIRECTIONS. TREATMENT DOSAGE: MIX 1 OZ CORID IN 5 OZ. WATER AND ORALLY DRENCH THE SICK GOATS TWICE A DAY FOR FIVE CONSECUTIVE DAYS; KIDS SHOULD RECEIVE 20-40 CC OF THIS MIXTURE TWICE A DAY, WHILE ADULTS SHOULD RECEIVE 40-80 CC. THIS IS A HIGHER-THAN-LABEL DOSAGE BUT IS WHAT IT TAKES TO CONTROL COCCIDIA IN GOATS. FOR PREVENTION OF COCCIDIA, USE 2 OZ. PER 15 GALLONS OF WATER; FOR TREATMENT, USE 3 OZ. CORID PER 15 GALLONS OF WATER. LIMIT THE GOATS' WATER SUPPLY TO ONE SOURCE AND TREAT FOR FIVE CONSECUTIVE DAYS. **USE THIAMINE (VITAMIN B1) DAILY DOSING AT 4 CC PER 100 LBS BODYWEIGHT GIVEN IM OR SQ WHEN USING CORID.**

CYLENCE

TOPICAL PRODUCT USED TO KILL LICE ON ADULT GOATS. CONTROLS HORN FLIES, FACE FLIES, BITING AND SUCKING LICE.
TO CONTROL FLIES, USE ONCE A MONTH THROUGHOUT THE SUMMER.
MILK WITHHOLDING TIME: NONE
NOTES: CONTAINS CYFLUTHRIN, A 4TH GENERATION PYRETHROID.

DOSAGE

POUR-ON - DRIP THIS ALONG THE GOAT'S SPINE. 1CC PER 25 POUNDS FOR LICE TREATMENT, REPEAT IN 3 WEEKS.

DEWORMERS, FEED-BASED

FEED-BASED DEWORMERS ARE USUALLY NOT EFFECTIVE. DEWORMERS ARE DOSED BASED ON THE GOAT'S BODYWEIGHT; THERE IS NO ACCURATE WAY TO DO THIS WITH FEED-BASED DEWORMERS. PLUS THE GOAT NEEDING THE DEWORMER THE WORST WILL ALSO BE THE LEAST AGGRESSIVE GOAT WHO WILL GET LESS FEED, THEREFORE A LOWER DOSAGE OF THE FEED-BASED DEWORMER. UNLESS YOU CAN CONTROL THE PRECISE AMOUNT OF FEED THAT EACH GOAT RECEIVES, I RECOMMEND AGAINST USING FEED-BASED DEWORMERS.

DEWORMERS

THERE ARE MULTIPLE CLASSES OF DEWORMERS. SOME STILL KILL STOMACH WORMS; MANY ARE NO LONGER EFFECTIVE. GENERALLY SPEAKING, THE WHITE-COLORED DEWORMERS (SAFEGUARD/PANACUR AND VALBAZEN) NO LONGER KILL STOMACH WORMS IN MUCH OF THE USA. ALL DEWORMERS SHOULD BE GIVEN ORALLY, REGARDLESS OF PACKAGE DIRECTIONS.

MEDICATIONS: A-Z

MEDICATIONS A-Z FOR SICKNESS & INJURY

 DEXAMETHASONE

VET PRESCRIPTION. CORTICO-STEROID. USE SPARINGLY AND UNDER THE DIRECTION OF A VET. DEX CAN HAVE BAD SIDE EFFECTS. USED FOR SWELLING AND INFLAMMATION AFTER INFECTION IS UNDER CONTROL. DO NOT USE IF BROKEN BONES EXIST; DEX INTERFERES WITH BONE REPAIR. DO NOT USE ON PREGNANT DOES UNLESS YOU ARE TRYING TO INDUCE LABOR. USED TO INDUCE LABOR IN PREGNANT DOES WHEN THE SLOW INTRODUCTION OF LABOR OVER A 48-TO-72 HOUR PERIOD IS DESIRED (PREGNANCY DISEASES LIKE PREGNANCY TOXEMIA & KETOSIS). DEX INTERFERES WITH THE FUNCTIONING OF THE GOAT'S IMMUNE SYSTEM. USAGE OF THIS DRUG MUST BE TAPERED OFF SLOWLY; SERIOUS PROBLEMS CAN OCCUR IF DEX IS GIVEN IN LARGE AMOUNTS AND THEN SUDDENLY STOPPED. TAPERING OFF OVER FIVE DAYS IS A NORMAL PROCEDURE, I.E. REDUCING THE DOSAGE EACH DAY FOR FIVE CONSECUTIVE DAYS. DOSAGE VARIES DEPENDING UPON THE PROBLEM BEING TREATED. KEEPS BEST IN HOT CLIMATES WHEN REFRIGERATED.

 DEXTROSE SOLUTION (50%)

THIS OVER-THE-COUNTER IV PRODUCT IN A BOTTLE IS USED ORALLY WITH WEAK NEWBORNS BY SLOWLY DROPPING ONE OR TWO CC IN THE MOUTH AND UNDER THE TONGUE FOR QUICK ENERGY. CAN BE MIXED HALF AND HALF WITH WATER AND OFFERED SHORT-TERM TO WEAK GOATS OR KIDS WHO ARE EITHER HAVING TROUBLE DIGESTING MILK OR HAVE OVEREATEN ON MILK (FLOPPY KID SYNDROME) AND NEED TO BE TAKEN OFF MILK FOR SEVERAL DAYS UNTIL THE TOXICITY CAUSED BY UNDIGESTED MILK HAS BEEN SUCCESSFULLY TREATED.

 DIATOMACEOUS EARTH (DE)

ALTHOUGH THIS PRODUCT IS BEING USED BY SOME PRODUCERS AS A "NATURAL" DEWORMER, DE DOES NOT KILL INTERNAL PARASITES (WORMS). THERE IS NO SCIENTIFIC EVIDENCE OF DE'S EFFECTIVENESS IN CONTROLLING INTERNAL PARASITES. EVERY CONTROLLED TEST DONE TO DETERMINE EFFICACY OF THIS PRODUCT IN KILLING INTERNAL PARASITES (WORMS) IN GOATS HAS FAILED. IT IS SOMEWHAT EFFECTIVE ON EXTERNAL PARASITES LIKE FLIES, FLEAS AND LICE. IF A PRODUCER CHOOSES TO USE DE AS A FOOD ADDITIVE, MAKE CERTAIN THAT "FOOD-GRADE" DE IS PURCHASED AND USE DE IN CONJUNCTION WITH AN ETHICAL (COMMERCIALLY-PRODUCED) DEWORMING PRODUCT. CHECK FECAL SAMPLES REGULARLY FOR WORMS WHILE USING DE. THERE IS NO SUCH THING AS A "NATURAL DEWORMER" FOR GOATS.

QUICK TIP

After any round of antibiotics, always replenish a goat's gut with probiotics.

MEDICATIONS A-Z FOR SICKNESS & INJURY

DOPRAM V

VET PRESCRIPTION. (MAY HAVE TO BE COMPOUNDED BY A PHARMACY AS IT MAY NO LONGER BE AVAILABLE COMMERCIALLY.) ELIMINATES RESPIRATORY DISTRESS IN NEWBORNS CAUSED BY TROUBLED BIRTHS, INCLUDING C-SECTIONS. USE ON "PULLED" KIDS SINCE THE NORMAL SQUEEZING OF THE BODY DURING THE DELIVERY PROCESS IS ALTERED. THIS LIQUID MEDICATION KEEPS BEST UNDER REFRIGERATION. THIS IS A MUST-HAVE MEDICATION.

DOSAGE

DROP 2/10 CC UNDER KID'S TONGUE IMMEDIATELY UPON BIRTH TO STIMULATE LUNG ACTIVITY.

DRAXXIN (TULOTHROMYCIN)

VET PRESCRIPTION. INJECTABLE RESPIRATORY ANTIBIOTIC. VERY EXPENSIVE PRODUCT THAT PURPORTS TO BE A ONE-TIME-ONLY USAGE ANTIBIOTIC. BECAUSE GOATS HAVE THE FASTEST METABOLISM OF ALL RUMINANTS, THEY NEED TO BE DOSED DAILY FOR FIVE DAYS.

DOSAGE
1.1 CC/100 LBS

DYNE

OVER-THE-COUNTER ORAL HIGH-CALORIE FOOD SUPPLEMENT FOR ANIMALS OFF FEED OR NEEDING QUICK ENERGY. MUST-HAVE PRODUCT.

ELECTROLYTES, ORAL

(BOUNCE BACK, RESORB, ENTROLYTE HE, OR EQUIVALENT) OVER-THE-COUNTER PRODUCTS PACKAGED IN POWERED FORM. OR USE THE RECIPE PROVIDED IN THIS BINDER. FOR REHYDRATING SICK ANIMALS, REGARDLESS OF AGE. CAN BE USED AS AN ORAL DRENCH, PUT INTO BABY BOTTLES FOR KIDS TO SUCK, OR MIXED IN DRINKING WATER. CAN BE USED IN CONJUNCTION WITH LACTATED RINGERS SOLUTION ON DEHYDRATED KIDS OR ADULTS. STORE IN A COOL, DRY PLACE. NEVER BE WITHOUT THIS PRODUCT.

ENTROLYTE

THIS TERRIFIC PRODUCT WAS PULLED BY PFIZER IN JANUARY 2008. IT WAS AN OVER-THE-COUNTER ORAL NUTRIENT PRODUCT FOR BOTH REHYDRATING AND PROVIDING NUTRITION TO RUMINANTS THAT WERE NOT RUMINATING OR OFF-FEED. CONTAINED 13+% PROTEIN IN ADDITION TO ELECTROLYTES. NO COMPARABLE REPLACEMENT PRODUCT IS ON THE MARKET, TO MY KNOWLEDGE. BEST ALTERNATIVE: MIX A PACKAGE OF ELECTROLYTES SUCH AS BOUNCE BACK OR RESORB AND ADD 8 TO 12 OZ MILK REPLACER.

MEDICATIONS: A-Z

MEDICATIONS A-Z FOR SICKNESS & INJURY

→ EPINEPHRINE

VET PRESCRIPTION. USED TO TREAT SHOCK. ALWAYS HAVE IT ON HAND WHEN GIVING INJECTIONS. SHOCK MUST BE TREATED WITHIN SECONDS OR THE GOAT WILL DIE.

DOSAGE
1 CC IM PER 100 POUNDS BODY WEIGHT.

→ EXCENEL RTU

PRESCRIPTION INJECTABLE ANTIBIOTIC. READY-TO-USE EQUIVALENT OF NAXCEL. EFFECTIVE AGAINST RESPIRATORY AND URINARY TRACT INFECTIONS.

DOSAGE
DOSE DAILY AT 6 CC PER 100 LBS BODYWEIGHT. DAY ONE: DOSE TWICE 12 HOURS APART. DAYS 2 THROUGH 5: DOSE ONCE DAILY. GIVE IM.

→ FERRODEX IRON INJECTABLE

OVER-THE-COUNTER INJECTABLE IRON SUPPLEMENT FOR TREATING ANEMIA. INTERCHANGEABLE WITH ORAL RED CELL OR ORAL LIXOTINIC. ORAL RED CELL IS PREFERRED.

→ FLEET'S ENEMA OR GENERIC EQUIVALENT

OVER-THE-COUNTER PRODUCT THAT IS USEFUL FOR CONSTIPATION AND TOXICITY REACTIONS TO CLEAN OUT THE INTESTINAL TRACT. IF A DOELING IS BORN WITH HER VAGINA TURNED INSIDE OUT, USE A CHILDREN'S FLEET'S ENEMA TO MOVE HER BOWELS FOR THE FIRST TIME ("PASS HER PLUG") AND THE VAGINA WILL RETURN TO ITS PROPER POSITION. MAKE SURE TO PUT THE ENEMA INTO THE RECTAL OPENING -- NOT THE VAGINA.

→ FORMALIN (10% BUFFERED FORMALDEHYDE)

CLASSIFIED AS A DISINFECTANT, THIS PRODUCT WORKS WELL WHEN INJECTED INTO CL ABSCESSES AND ALSO IS VERY EFFECTIVE IN TREATING HOOF ROT/HOOF SCALD. HOWEVER, IT MUST BE USED CORRECTLY!!

→ FORTIFIED VITAMIN B COMPLEX

OVER-THE-COUNTER PRODUCT. THIS PRODUCT CAN BE USED INSTEAD OF THIAMINE SINCE IT HAS 100 MG/ML THIAMINE IN IT. PRODUCTS WITHOUT "FORTIFIED" IN THE LABEL HAVE INADEQUATE LEVELS OF THIAMINE. IF SUCH PRODUCTS MUST BE USED, THEN THE DOSAGE MUST BE INCREASED TO ACHIEVE A THIAMINE LEVEL OF 100 MG/ML.
EXAMPLE: IF THE PRODUCT HAS ONLY 25 MG/ML THIAMINE, THEN THE DOSAGE GIVEN MUST BE MULTIPLIED BY FOUR. B VITAMINS ARE WATER SOLUBLE; A HEALTHY RUMEN PRODUCES B VITAMINS DAILY.

DOSAGE
DOSAGE IS 4 CC PER 100 POUNDS BODYWEIGHT.

MEDICATIONS A-Z FOR SICKNESS & INJURY

→ GENTAMYCIN SULFATE

INJECTABLE PRESCRIPTION ANTIBIOTIC. NOT AUTHORIZED FOR USE IN ALL JURISDICTIONS IN FOOD ANIMALS DUE TO CONCERN FOR ANTIBIOTIC RESIDUE IN MEAT. WORKS EXTREMELY WELL WHEN USED IN CONJUNCTION WITH PENICILLIN IN THE TREATMENT OF POST-BIRTHING INFECTIONS AND OTHER BACTERIAL INFECTIONS. MIXED IN EQUAL PARTS WITH DEXAMETHAZONE AND STERILE WATER, THE RESULTING PRODUCT IS A VERY EFFECTIVE EYE SPRAY FOR TREATING PINKEYE. DO NOT USE ON ULCERATED EYES.

→ GENTOSIN SPRAY

TOPICAL PRESCRIPTION SPRAY USEFUL IN TREATING PINKEYE IN NON-ULCERATED EYES. SEE GENTAMYCIN SULFATE.

→ GOAT NUTRIDRENCH

ORAL QUICK ENERGY SUPPLEMENT FOR STRESSED AND/OR OFF-FEED GOATS. CONTAINS MANY OF THE VITAMINS, MINERALS, AND NUTRIENTS THAT A SICK GOAT REQUIRES TO SURVIVE ITS ILLNESS. MIXES WELL WITH PROPYLENE GLYCOL OR MINERAL OIL FOR FLAVORED DOSING.

→ GRANULEX

TOPICAL SPRAY FOR REMOVING DEAD & DYING SKIN. MAY NOT BE AVAILABLE. CHECK WITH VET.

→ IMMODIUM AD

DO NOT USE THIS ANTI-DIARRHEAL WITH GOATS. IT CAN STOP THE PERISTALTIC ACTION OF THE GUT, CAUSING RAPID AND PAINFUL DEATH.

→ IVOMEC 1% INJECTABLE DEWORMER OR GENERIC EQUIVALENT INVERMECTIN

OVER-THE-COUNTER PRODUCT FOR ELIMINATING STOMACH WORMS. DO NOT UNDER-DOSE. STORE AT COOL TEMPERATURE AND KEEP OUT OF SUNLIGHT. ACHIEVES A QUICKER "KILL" VIA ORAL DOSING. ALSO USED IN TREATMENT OF MENINGEAL DEERWORM INFECTION. CLEAR DEWORMERS DO NOT KILL TAPEWORMS. IVERMECTIN 1% IS ONE OF SEVERAL DEWORMERS USED TO KILL STOMACH WORMS. ALL DEWORMERS SHOULD BE GIVEN ORALLY TO GOATS.

DOSAGE

THIS CLEAR LIQUID WORKS BEST IF USED ORALLY AT A RATE OF 1 CC PER 35 POUNDS BODY WEIGHT.

→ KOPERTOX

OVER-THE-COUNTER PRODUCT FOR HOOF ROT AND HOOF SCALD. BLUE-GREEN LIQUID FOR TOPICAL APPLICATION AS A "LIQUID BANDAGE." ALSO USE WITH OXYTETRACYCLINE 200 MG/ML INJECTIONS.

MEDICATIONS A-Z FOR SICKNESS & INJURY

LA 200, MAXIM 200, BIOMYCIN (OXYTETRACYLINE 200 MG/ML)

OVER-THE-COUNTER BROAD-SPECTRUM ANTIBIOTIC. THICK (USE AN 18 GAUGE NEEDLE AND GIVE SQ OVER THE RIBS) AND MAY STING. OXYTRETRACYCLINE 200 MG/ML MUST BE USED TO TREAT ABORTION "STORMS." NO VACCINES ARE AVAILABLE TO TREAT ABORTION DISEASES AND NO OFF-LABEL VACCINES ARE EFFECTIVE IN PREVENTING ABORTION DISEASES IN GOATS. OXYTETRACYCLINE 200 MG/ML IS THE GOAT PRODUCER'S ONLY CHOICE. ALSO USED TO TREAT PINKEYE, EVEN IN PREGNANT DOES, AS AN ABORTION ORGANISM CAN CAUSE ONE STRAIN OF PINKEYE. USED BOTH INJECTABLY AND TOPICALLY (IN NON-ULCERATED EYES) FOR PINKEYE. SOMETIMES EFFECTIVE IN TREATING HOOF ROT/HOOF SCALD INFECTIONS. THE NON-STING VERSION OF OXYTETRACYCLINE 200 MG/ML IS CALLED BIOMYCIN. OXYTETRACYCLINE 200 MG/ML IS SOLD UNDER SEVERAL BRAND NAMES; CHECK THE CONTENT LABEL FOR CORRECT 200 MG/ML STRENGTH. TURNS A DARK RED WHEN OPENED AND AIR ENTERS THE BOTTLE, BUT IF KEPT UNDER CONTROLLED CLIMATIC CONDITIONS AND USED BEFORE THE EXPIRATION DATE, IT SHOULD WORK FINE.

DOSAGE

USE 1 CC PER 20 LBS. BODY WEIGHT SQ DAILY FOR A MINIMUM OF FIVE CONSECUTIVE DAYS.

LACTATED RINGERS SOLUTION

VET PRESCRIPTION. FOR REHYDRATING KIDS AND YOUNG GOATS. COMES IN IV BAG BUT USE SQ. USING A 60 CC SYRINGE WITH AN 18 GAUGE NEEDLE ATTACHED, DRAW UP LRS, WARM IN A POT OF WATER, CHECK TEMPERATURE AS YOU WOULD A BOTTLE OF MILK FOR PROPER HEAT, AND INJECT 30 CC UNDER THE SKIN (SQ) AT EACH SHOULDER. CAN BE USED SEVERAL TIMES A DAY UNTIL THE GOAT'S ELECTROLYTES ARE IN BALANCE. WILL BE ABSORBED BY THE GOAT'S BODY VERY QUICKLY IF DEHYDRATION IS PRESENT. CAN BE USED IN CONJUNCTION WITH ORAL ELECTROLYTES (BOUNCEBACK/RESORB). REFRIGERATE WHEN STORING OR STRANGE THINGS WILL GROW INSIDE THE BAG. A MUST-HAVE PRODUCT.

DOSAGE

30 CC UNDER THE SKIN (SQ) AT EACH SHOULDER

LIME SULPHUR DIP 97.8%

USED TOPICALLY FOR MITES AND STAPH INFECTIONS ON THE SKIN.

LUTALYSE

PRESCRIPTION INJECTABLE. USED TO CYCLE DOES INTO HEAT OR INDUCE ABORTION IN DOE BRED TO WRONG BUCK OR BRED TOO EARLY.

DOSAGE

GIVE 2 CC ON THE SEVENTH (7TH) DAY AFTER OBSERVED BREEDING. DO NOT REPEAT.

MEDICATIONS: A-Z

MEDICATIONS A-Z FOR SICKNESS & INJURY

→ MARQUIS
SEE TOLTRAZURIL FOR COST-EFFECTIVE ALTERNATIVE.

→ MASTI-CLEAR
PROCAINE-PENICILLIN-BASED TEAT INFUSION FOR LACTATING DOES TO TREAT MASTITIS.

→ MICOTIL
NEVER USE MICOTIL ON GOATS. CATTLE ANTIBIOTIC CAUSES QUICK HEART ATTACK AND DEATH.

→ MILK OF MAGNESIA
OVER-THE-COUNTER LAXATIVE PRODUCT THAT IS USEFUL FOR CONSTIPATION AND TOXICITY REACTIONS (TO MOVE TOXIC MATERIALS FROM THE BODY), INCLUDING BLOAT, RUMINAL ACIDOSIS, OVEREATING DISEASE, AND FLOPPY KID SYNDROME. ALWAYS KEEP THE ANIMAL HYDRATED WITH ELECTROLYTES (BOUNCEBACK/RESORB OR EQUIVALENT) WHEN USING MILK OF MAGNESIA OR OTHER LAXATIVES. USEFUL WITH MASTITIS BY INCREASING MAGNESIUM LEVELS IN GOAT'S BODY. KEEP "MOM" ON HAND AT ALL TIMES.

DOSAGE
USE AS ORAL DRENCH AT A RATE OF 15 CC PER 60 LBS. BODY WEIGHT EVERY FOUR TO SIX HOURS UNTIL THE FECES GOES FROM NORMAL TO CLUMPY THEN BACK TO NORMAL ROUND BALLS.

→ MINERAL MAX (MULTI MIN)
VET PRESCRIPTION. COBALT-BLUE COLORED INJECTABLE LIQUID THAT **MUST BE USED SPARINGLY IN GOATS** SUFFERING FROM SEVERE MINERAL DEFICIENCIES. HELP WITH WEAK LABOR CONTRACTIONS. OVERDOSING IS EASY; THIS MEDICATION BUILDS UP IN FATTY TISSUES. DOSE SQ ONLY.

→ MINERAL OIL
OVER-THE-COUNTER LAXATIVE PRODUCT. BECAUSE MINERAL OIL HAS NO TASTE, THE GOAT DOES NOT RECOGNIZE MINERAL OIL AS A SUBSTANCE TO BE SWALLOWED AND CAN ASPIRATE IT INTO THE LUNGS. MUST BE STOMACH TUBED. IF STOMACH TUBE IS NOT IMMEDIATELY AVAILABLE, MIX MINERAL OIL WITH GOAT NUTRIDRENCH TO FLAVOR IT AND SLOWLY ORALLY DRENCH INTO THE GOAT'S MOUTH.

→ MOLASSES/KARO SYRUP
USE ORALLY WITH KIDS WHEN QUICK ENERGY IS NEEDED. CAN BE SUBSTITUTED FOR PROPYLENE GLYCOL WITH KETOTIC DOES. SEE RECIPE IN PROVIDED IN THIS BINDER.
DOSAGE
1/4 CUP TO 1/2 CUP TO ONE GALLON OF WATER

→ NALALGEN IP
INTRA-NASAL VACCINE OF SHORT DURATION. CAN BE ADMINISTERED TO GOATS WHEN SHIPPING.

MEDICATIONS A-Z FOR SICKNESS & INJURY

➤ NAXCEL (CEFTIOFUR SODIUM)

VET PRESCRIPTION. BROAD-SPECTRUM ANTIBIOTIC USED FOR RESPIRATORY ILLNESSES (PNEUMONIA). COMES IN TWO BOTTLES: ONE BOTTLE CONTAINS A POWDER WHICH MUST BE KEPT REFRIGERATED EVEN IN POWDER FORM, AND THE OTHER BOTTLE IS STERILE WATER. WHEN THE TWO ARE MIXED, THEY KEEP FOR ONLY SEVEN DAYS. DRAW SYRINGES IN DOSAGES OF 1/2 CC, 1 CC, 2 CC, AND 3 CC, PUT NEEDLE CAPS ON THEM, PLACE THE FILLED SYRINGES IN A ZIPLOCK BAG, LABEL AND DATE IT, AND PUT THE BAG IN THE FREEZER. SYRINGES THAW QUICKLY, BUT HOLD THE NEEDLE CAP UPRIGHT, BECAUSE THE MEDICATION WILL SETTLE INTO THE NEEDLE CAP AND WILL BE LOST WHEN THE NEEDLE CAP IS REMOVED. EXCENEL RTU IS THE READY-TO-USE EQUIVALENT PRODUCT THAT DOESN'T REQUIRE REFRIGERATION OR MIXING, OR NUFLOR GOLD.

DOSAGE

NEWBORN KIDS WITH RESPIRATORY DISTRESS OR E.COLI INFECTIONS NEED A MINIMUM DOSAGE IM OF 1/2 CC DAILY FOR FIVE CONSECUTIVE DAYS. A 100 POUND GOAT NEEDS AT LEAST 5-6 CC OF NAXCEL IM OVER THE FIVE-DAY COURSE OF TREATMENT.

➤ NIACIN (VITAMIN B3)

GIVE 1000 MG DAILY ORALLY (CRUSHED AND DISSOLVED) TO DOES HAVING WEAK LABOR CONTRACTIONS UNTIL KIDDING OCCURS.

➤ NOLVASAN

BOLUS USED INSIDE UTERUS AFTER DIFFICULT DELIVERY TO PREVENT METRITIS OR VAGINITIS.

➤ NUFLOR GOLD (FLORFENICOL)

VET PRESCRIPTION. A GOOD PRODUCT FOR RESPIRATORY PROBLEMS, INCLUDING PNEUMONIA. CAN ALSO BE USED TO TRY TO KEEP MASTITIS FROM BECOMING SYSTEMIC. I TEND TO USE NUFLOR ON ADULTS AND EXCENEL RTU ON KIDS, BUT THEY ARE INTERCHANGEABLE. THIS IS A THICK LIQUID, SO USE LUER LOCK SYRINGES, OR THE NEEDLE MAY BLOW OFF THE SYRINGE. KEEPS BEST UNDER REFRIGERATION IN WARM CLIMATES.

DOSAGE

6 CC PER 100 LBS BODYWEIGHT GIVEN IM FOR FIVE CONSECUTIVE DAYS; NEWBORN KIDS SHOULD RECEIVE NO LESS THAN 1/2 CC.

➤ OXYTOCIN

VET PRESCRIPTION. USED WHEN A DOE HAS NOT PASSED HER AFTERBIRTH WITHIN 24-36 HOURS OF KIDDING. IN WARM CLIMATES, KEEPS BEST WHEN REFRIGERATED.

DOSAGE

1-1/2 CC PER 100 LBS BODY WEIGHT.

MEDICATIONS A-Z FOR SICKNESS & INJURY

➔ PENICLLIN, BENZATHINE (LONG-ACTING PENICILLIN)

OVER-THE-COUNTER ANTIBIOTIC. HAS BEEN OVERUSED AND IS OFTEN NO LONGER EFFECTIVE. MUST BE REFRIGERATED. DO NOT USE THIS TYPE OF PENICILLIN IF LISTERIOSIS OR GOAT POLIO IS SUSPECTED. I DON'T KEEP THIS PENICILLIN IN STOCK ANY LONGER.

DOSAGE
5 CC PER 100 LBS. BODY WEIGHT IM FOR FIVE CONSECUTIVE DAYS.

➔ PENICILLIN, PROCAINE (300,000 IU)

PROCAINE PENICILLIN MUST BE USED IN HIGHER THAN USUAL DOSAGES IN CONJUNCTION WITH THIAMINE (VITAMIN B1) IN THE TREATMENT OF LISTERIOSIS AND GOAT POLIO. ALSO IS USED TO TREAT INFECTION RESULTING FROM INJURIES, BITES, AND AFTER DIFFICULT BIRTHINGS. OVER-THE-COUNTER PRODUCT. MUST BE REFRIGERATED. ALWAYS HAVE LOTS OF THIS PRODUCT ON HAND.

DOSAGE
1CC/ 20 LBS, SQ INJECTION FOR 5 DAYS. USE A 16 OR 18 GAUGE NEEDLE

➔ PEPPERMINT OIL CREAM (CAI-PAN)

TOPICAL APPLICATION FOR CONGESTED AND/OR MASTITIC UDDERS.

➔ PEPTO BISMOL (PINK BISMUTH)

OVER-THE-COUNTER PRODUCT TO HELP WITH IRRITATION/DISTRESS CAUSED BY DIARRHEA IN BOTH KIDS AND ADULTS. BEFORE USING PEPTO-BISMOL WHEN DIARRHEA IS PRESENT, FIRST DETERMINE THE CAUSE OF THE PROBLEM.

DOSAGE
USE UP TO 2 CC EVERY FOUR TO SIX HOURS FOR NEWBORNS; 5 CC FOR KIDS APPROACHING ONE MONTH OLD; AS MUCH AS 10 TO 15 CC FOR ADULTS.

➔ PIRSUE

VET PRESCRIPTION MASTITIS MEDICATION. EXPENSIVE BUT EXCELLENT PRODUCT.

➔ PEPTO BISMOL (PINK BISMUTH)

OVER-THE-COUNTER PRODUCT TO HELP WITH IRRITATION/DISTRESS CAUSED BY DIARRHEA IN BOTH KIDS AND ADULTS. BEFORE USING PEPTO-BISMOL WHEN DIARRHEA IS PRESENT, FIRST DETERMINE THE CAUSE OF THE PROBLEM.

DOSAGE
USE UP TO 2 CC EVERY FOUR TO SIX HOURS FOR NEWBORNS; 5 CC FOR KIDS APPROACHING ONE MONTH OLD; AS MUCH AS 10 TO 15 CC FOR ADULTS.

MEDICATIONS A-Z FOR SICKNESS & INJURY

→ PNEUMONIA VACCINES: PRESPONSE HM AND POLY BAC SOMNUS

BOTH VACCINES ARE NEWER AND PROVIDE BETTER PROTECTION AGAINST PNEUMONIA THAN THE COLORADO SERUM PRODUCT MENTIONED BELOW; THEY ARE ALSO MORE EXPENSIVE. THE EXTRA COST IS REDUCED BY THE LESSER AMOUNT OF VACCINE NEEDED FOR THE 60 LB & UNDER GOATS. IF PNEUMONIA IS A PROBLEM IN YOUR HERD, USE THESE NEWER PRODUCTS.

DOSAGE

1 CC FOR GOATS UNDER 60 LBS AND 2 CC FOR GOATS OVER 60 LBS, WITH A TWO-INJECTION SERIES 21 DAYS APART THE FIRST TIME AND ANNUALLY THEREAFTER.

→ PNEUMONIA VACCINE (MANNHEIMIA HAEMOLYTICA PASTEURELLA MULTOCIDE BACTERIN)

OVER-THE-COUNTER INJECTABLE PNEUMONIA VACCINE BY COLORADO SERUM. MADE FOR GOATS. GIVE FIRST INJECTION IN CONJUNCTION WITH FIRST DEWORMING AND FIRST CD/T VACCINATION. REPEAT 30 DAYS LATER THEN ANNUALLY THEREAFTER.

DOSAGE

REQUIRES TWO INITIAL INJECTIONS OF 2 CC EACH 30 DAYS APART FOR ALL YOUNG GOATS AND ANY NEW PURCHASES BROUGHT ONTO THE PROPERTY REGARDLESS OF AGE, THEN BOOSTER ANNUALLY THEREAFTER. DOSAGE IS 2 CC FOR ALL GOATS, REGARDLESS OF AGE, SEX, WEIGHT, OR BREED.

→ POLYSERUM OR BOVI SERA

OVER-THE-COUNTER INJECTABLE IMMUNE SYSTEM BOOSTERS. GIVE SQ. USE WITH ANY ILL OR UNTHRIFTY GOAT. GIVE TO YOUNG KIDS THAT DID NOT RECEIVE ADEQUATE COLOSTRUM.

→ PRIMOR (SULFADIMETHOXINE & ORMETOPRIM IN 5:1 RATIO)

VET PRESCRIPTION. ORAL SULFA-BASED ANTIBIOTIC. TABLETS SIZED BY WEIGHT OF ANIMAL FOR GUT-RELATED INFECTIONS, INCLUDING COCCIDIOSIS. TABLETS ARE SCORED BY ANIMAL WEIGHT FOR EASY DOSING. PRIMOR 120 IS FOR 5-15 LB GOATS; PRIMOR 240, 10-30 LB GOATS; PRIMOR 600, 25-50 LB GOATS; AND PRIMOR 1200, 50-100 LB GOATS. GIVE TWO TIMES THE APPROPRIATE WEIGHT'S DOSAGE THE FIRST DAY, AND THEN DOSE TO THE GOAT'S WEIGHT FOR THE NEXT 9 CONSECUTIVE DAYS.

→ PROBIOTICS, ORAL

OVER-THE-COUNTER ORAL RUMINANT GEL WHICH SHOULD BE USED AFTER THE COMPLETION OF ANTIBIOTIC THERAPY, TREATMENT FOR DIARRHEA (SCOURS), AND DAILY WHEN GOATS ARE IN SHIPMENT. HELPS LESSEN STRESS AND SETTLE THE STOMACH. KEEP REFRIGERATED IN WARM CLIMATES.

MEDICATIONS A-Z FOR SICKNESS & INJURY

➤ PROPLYENE GLYCOL

OVER-THE-COUNTER LIQUID FOR KETOSIS IN DOES. PROVIDES QUICK ENERGY. COMES IN ONE-GALLON JUGS. MIX WITH GOAT NUTRIDRENCH SO THE GOAT CAN TASTE IT AND KNOW TO SWALLOW. IF THIS PRODUCT IS NOT AVAILABLE, USE MOLASSES OR KARO SYRUP. FREEZES AT TEMPERATURES WELL ABOVE 32*F, SO STORE INDOORS UNDER CONTROLLED TEMPERATURE.

DOSAGE

USE 50-60 CC ORALLY VERY SLOWLY TWICE A DAY FOR AN AVERAGE-SIZED ADULT DOE UNTIL SHE BEGINS EATING.

➤ RALLY OR RECOVR

INJECTABLE ANTIHISTAMINE FOR TOXICITY PROBLEMS. VET PRESCRIPTION.

➤ RED CELL

OVER-THE-COUNTER FLAVORED ORAL IRON SUPPLEMENT MADE FOR HORSES. USED IN TREATING ANEMIA.

DOSAGE

4 CC ORALLY GIVEN DAILY.

➤ SAFEGUARD (PANACUR) DEWORMER

WHITE-COLORED DEWORMER. NO LONGER KILLS STOMACH WORMS IN MOST OF USA. USED TO KILL TAPEWORMS AND MENINGEAL DEER WORM INFECTION. DUE TO RESISTANCE IN PARASITES, SAFEGUARD IS NOT EFFECTIVE IN MOST LOCATIONS. WITHHOLD MILK FOR 2 WEEKS.

DOSAGE

1 CC/ 10 LBS, GIVEN ORALLY.

➤ SPECTAM SCOUR HALT

OVER-THE-COUNTER SULFA-BASED ANTIBIOTIC PRODUCT TO CONTROL DIARRHEA IN KIDS. USAGE WITH ADULT GOATS MAY STOP THE PERISTALTIC ACTION OF THE GUT.

DOSAGE

FOLLOW LABEL DIRECTIONS WHEN DOSING THIS PINKISH-RED LIQUID INTO THE GOAT'S MOUTH. 1 CC PER 10 POUNDS.

➤ STERILE WATER

VET PRESCRIPTION. USED IN MIXING MEDICATIONS.

QUICK TIP

Make a habit to check your goat's eyelids on a weekly basis. Stay ahead of anemia!

MEDICATIONS: A-Z

MEDICATIONS A-Z FOR SICKNESS & INJURY

SULFADIMETHOXAZINE WITH TRIMETHOPRIM (SMZ)

SULFA-BASED ORAL PRESCRIPTION ANTIBIOTIC. AVAILABLE IN LIQUID AND TABLETS. USE TO TREAT WATERY DIARRHEA AND OTHER GUT-RELATED ILLNESSES. USED WITH BAYTRIL 100, SMZ IS SYNERGISTIC (BETTER THAN BY ITSELF) IN TREATING E COLI AND OTHER DIFFICULT TO CURE INFECTIONS. EXCELLENT PRODUCT.

SYNERGIZED DELICE OR GENERIC EQUIVALENT

*SYNERGIZED DELICE OR GENERIC EQUIVALENT - OVER-THE-COUNTER PRODUCT. THIS PERMETHRIN-BASED OILY LIQUID SHOULD BE APPLIED TOPICALLY ALONG THE BACKBONE FROM BASE OF NECK TO BASE OF TAIL. (THIS BACK DRENCH WORKS ON GOATS BECAUSE EXTERNAL PARASITES ARE THE TARGET; BACK DRENCHES DON'T WORK FOR TREATING INTERNAL PARASITES LIKE STOMACH WORMS.) FOLLOW THE DIRECTIONS CAREFULLY, AND DO NOT USE ON KIDS UNDER 3 MONTHS OF AGE AND PREGNANT DOES. TOPICAL BACK DRENCH DOSAGE SHOULD NEVER EXCEED 3 OUNCES ON THE BIGGEST AND HEAVIEST OF GOATS. USE A RECLAIMED PERMANENT SQUEEZE BOTTLE WITH APPLICATOR TIP TO APPLY THIS PRODUCT. THE BOTTLE TIP IS JUST THE RIGHT SIZE. FOR KIDS UNDER THREE MONTHS OF AGE AND PREGNANT DOES, USE A KITTEN-SAFE OR PUPPY-SAFE POWDERED FLEA CONTROL PRODUCT OR CAREFULLY APPLY 5% SEVIN DUST. THESE PRODUCTS CONTAIN PYRETHRINS, WHICH ARE MUCH SAFER FOR VERY YOUNG ANIMALS. **CYLENCE IS A COMPARABLE TOPICAL PRODUCT USED TO KILL LICE ON ADULT GOATS.***

TAGAMET

OVER-THE-COUNTER PRODUCT FOR GUT-RELATED PAIN RESULTING FROM ILLNESSES LIKE COCCIDIOSIS.

DOSAGE

ONE HALF OF A TAGAMET HR200 (200 MG) FOR 3-5 DAYS.

TERRAMYCIN

OVER-THE-COUNTER PRODUCT. OPTHALMIC OINTMENT USED TO TREAT PINKEYE, PARTICULARLY IN ULCERATED EYES.

TETANUS ANTI-TOXIN

OVER-THE-COUNTER PRODUCT FOR IMMEDIATE AND SHORT-TERM PROTECTION AGAINST TETANUS (LOCKJAW) WHEN THE PROBLEM EXISTS. TETANUS IS FATAL IF NOT PROMPTLY TREATED. COMES IN SINGLE-DOSE 1500 UNIT VIALS; USE THE ENTIRE 1500 UNIT VIAL IM FOR ADULTS; USE HALF THE 1500 UNIT VIAL FOR KIDS. NO SOONER THAN FIVE DAYS AFTER THIS MEDICATION IS LAST USED, YOU MUST RE-VACCINATE WITH TETANUS TOXOID OR CD/T (THE COMPLETE TWO-INJECTION SERIES GIVEN 30 DAYS APART) TO REINSTATE LONG-TERM PROTECTION. KEEP REFRIGERATED.

MEDICATIONS: A-Z

MEDICATIONS A-Z FOR SICKNESS & INJURY

THEODUR
VET PRESCRIPTION. USED TO CLEAR AIR PASSAGES WHEN BRONCHITIS EXISTS. PRECISE DOSAGE IS NOT KNOWN FOR GOATS, USE UNDER VET DIRECTION AND SUPERVISION, 1/2 TABLET PER DAY ON A 15-20 POUND KID CAN BE USED. THEODUR SUPPRESSES THE APPETITE; THE PRODUCER MUST MAKE SURE THAT THE ANIMAL IS KEPT HYDRATED.

THIAMINE (VITAMIN B1)
VET PRESCRIPTION. USED WITH ANY GOAT THAT IS OFF-FEED. ALSO USED TO TREAT GOAT POLIO AND LISTERIOSIS. KEEPS BEST IN WARM CLIMATES WHEN REFRIGERATED.

DOSAGE
4 CC PER 100 POUNDS BODYWEIGHT UP TO THREE TIMES PER DAY IM, OR SQ.

THRUSH BUSTER
TOPICAL PRODUCT TO TREAT AND PREVENT HOOF SCALD (BETWEEN TOES).

TODAY (CEPHAPIRIN SODIUM)-
OVER-THE-COUNTER PRODUCT FOR MASTITIS TREATMENT IN LACTATING DOES. MILK OUT THE UDDER AND INFUSE ONE TUBE OF TO-DAY INTO EACH TEAT FOR THREE TO FIVE CONSECUTIVE DAYS. USE THE ALCOHOL WIPE PROVIDED TO CLEAN THE TEAT THOROUGHLY BEFORE INFUSING MEDICATION TO AVOID INTRODUCING NEW BACTERIA INTO AN ALREADY-INFECTED UDDER.

TOLTRAZURIL
THIS IS A CLOSE "RELATIVE" OF THE VERY EXPENSIVE MARQUIS FOR TREATING COCCIDIOSIS. CURRENTLY BEING BOUGHT ONLINE FROM WWW.HORSEPREPRACE.COM. THIS IS NOT AN ENDORSEMENT OF THIS PRODUCT OR THIS SUPPLIER.

DOSAGE
DOSING ONE TIME AT ONE CC PER FIVE POUNDS BODY WEIGHT

TOMORROW (CEPHAPIRIN BENZATHINE)
OVER-THE-COUNTER TREATMENT FOR MASTITIS IN DRY DOES.

TRIPLE ANTIBIOTIC OPTHALMIC OINTMENT
VET PRESCRIPTION. USE TOPICALLY TO TREAT PINKEYE, PARTICULARLY IN ULCERATED EYES.

TYLAN 200 (TYLOSIN)
PRESCRIPTION ANTIBIOTIC FOR RESPIRATORY PROBLEMS. KEEPS BEST IN WARM CLIMATES WHEN REFRIGERATED. THE PRESCRIPTION PRODUCTS NUFLOR GOLD AND EXCENEL RTU ARE FAR MORE EFFECTIVE THAN TYLAN 200.

DOSAGE
1 CC PER 25 LBS. BODY WEIGHT FOR FIVE CONSECUTIVE DAYS INTRAMUSCULARLY (IM).

MEDICATIONS: A-Z

MEDICATIONS A-Z FOR SICKNESS & INJURY

→ **UNIVERSAL ANIMAL ANTIDOTE GEL**
GIVE ORALLY WHEN TOXICITY IS SUSPECTED OR DIAGNOSED.

→ **VALBAZEN**
OVER-THE-COUNTER WHITE-COLORED DEWORMER. CAN CAUSE ABORTIONS IN PREGNANT DOES IF USED IN FIRST TRIMESTER OF PREGNANCY. FOR SAFETY, NEVER USE ON PREGNANT DOES. DOES KILL TAPEWORMS.

   DOSAGE
   DOSAGE IS 1 CC PER 25 LBS. BODYWEIGHT GIVEN ORALLY.

→ **VITAMIN B1 (THIAMINE)**
VET PRESCRIPTION. SEE THIAMINE FOR USES AND DOSAGES.

→ **VITAMINE B-12**
VET PRESCRIPTION. THIS RED-COLORED INJECTABLE LIQUID IS ESSENTIAL FOR USE WITH GOATS WHO ARE ANEMIC FROM WORMS. ALSO STIMULATES APPETITE. KEEPS BEST REFRIGERATED.

   DOSAGE
   ADMINISTER 4 CC PER 100 LBS. BODY WEIGHT IM.

QUICK TIP

An ounce of prevention is worth a pound of cure.

CARE OF GOATS

THE TASKS OF GOAT OWNERSHIP

DAILY CARE

- FEED
- WATER CHECK (AND REFILLING IF NEEDED)
- MILKING
- MINERAL AND BAKING SODA CHECK
- ALWAYS USE 5 SENSES-OBSERVE!

WEEKLY CARE

- REFILL MINERAL & BAKING SODA
- DISINFECT FEEDING TROUGHS
- CLEAN & DISINFECT WATER TROUGHS, FILL
- CHECK FENCES FOR WEAK AREAS
- CHECK EYE COLOR (REFER TO COLOR CHART)
    - DARK PINK--EXCELLENT!
    - LIGHT PINK--ACT!
        - REFRESH MEMORY ABOUT ANEMIA SYMPTOMS
        - DEWORM
        - GIVE A SHOT OF B VITAMINS
    - PALE PINK--ACT QUICKLY!
        - BEGIN TREATING FOR ANEMIA IMMEDIATELY
        - DEWORM
        - GIVE A SHOT OF B VITAMINS
- CHECK GENERAL BODY CONDITION
- GIVE WEEKLY HERBAL WORM PREVANTATIVE

CARE OF GOATS

THE TASKS OF GOAT OWNERSHIP

MONTHLY CARE

- CHECK HOOVES, TRIM IF NEEDED
- RESTOCK GRAIN & LOW SUPPLIES
- CLEAN UP BARN AREA
  - REMOVE MANURE & SOILED BEDDING & OLD, RUINED HAY
  - STRAIGHTEN UP MEDICAL SUPPLIES, RESTOCK IF NEEDED
  - REPAIR ANYTHING BROKEN
- CLEAN UP OUTSIDE PEN AREAS
  - REMOVE MANURE & SOILED HAY
  - REPAIR ANY BROKEN FENCING OR BROKEN AREAS ON SHELTERS.

YEARLY CARE

- DETERMINE IF YOUR GOATS WILL NEED SUPPLEMENTS & HOW OFTEN
  - COPPER BOLUSES
  - SELENIUM
- DETERMINE IF YOU WILL GIVE CDT, PNEUMONIA OR ANY OTHER SHOTS
- PLAN WHAT YOU WILL REPAIR & BUILD IN THE NEXT YEAR
- DEEP CLEAN BARNS, SHELTERS & MILKING AREAS
- MARK CALENDARS:
  - BREEDING
  - KIDDING
  - WEANING
  - SHOTS
  - SUPPLEMENTS
  - DEEP CLEANING

MY
Goat
BINDER

CPSIA information can be obtained
at www.ICGtesting.com
Printed in the USA
LVHW060002140322
713096LV00001B/1

9 780578 540184